S

Making the Word

MAKING THE WORDS ACCEPTABLE

*The Shape of the Sermon in
Christian History*

Jonathan Hustler

 EPWORTH

British Library Cataloguing in Publication data

A catalogue record for this book is available
from the British Library

978 0 7162 0650 7

Extracts from Psalm 19 in Chapter 2 are from The Book of
Common Prayer of the Episcopal Church of the USA.

Other scripture quotations are from the New Revised Standard
Version of the Bible, copyright © 1989, 1995 by the Division of
Christian Education of the National Council of the Churches of
Christ in the USA. Used by permission. All rights reserved.

First published in 2009
by Epworth
Methodist Church House
25 Marylebone Road
London NW1 5JR

Typeset by Regent Typesetting, London
Printed in Great Britain by
MPG Books, Bodmin, Cornwall

CONTENTS

PREFACE

A visitor to London can find far worse ways to spend a wet afternoon than by visiting the National Portrait Gallery. The collection is divided between four floors; starting at the top, viewers work their way chronologically down the stairs. Moving from century to century the viewer notices that the portraits are often stylized. Compare, for instance, what are probably the oldest portraits – those of kings Henry IV, Edward IV and Richard III. All three appear in the same pose, with only the top half of the body seen. In all three pictures the centre of attention is the head, and the fingers are adorned with rings, indicating the wealth and status of the sitter. This, clearly, is what a king was expected to look like, and not simply a stylistic choice by the artist. Much portraiture is commissioned; in some way or other it is a response to expectation, and the first gallery of the National Portrait Gallery clearly shows that when someone in the sixteenth century thought of a portrait, that was what he or she expected.

Expectations had clearly changed by the late seventeenth century. The portraits become more elaborate, more heroic. Subjects are presented astride horses or in elaborate regalia or ceremonial dress. In the late eighteenth century this is developed further, with classical types being used to express the particular virtue of the sitter. The twentieth-century collection reveals a range of attitudes, with a greater realism than in any previous period, but also with a clear desire from the artist to capture something of the inner character of the sitter. So, to sum up in an unscientific way (and as someone who claims no expertise at all in the history of art) one moves through the portrait gallery from those pictures in which the emphasis is on the office of the person, through those in which the achievements are celebrated, to those which are about the person per se. Yet on each floor the portraits are styled according to what those who painted them and those who commissioned them would have expected a portrait to be.

Preaching a sermon can be likened to painting a portrait. A sermon presents a picture of somebody. That somebody might be Jesus Christ or it might be God the Holy Trinity. Conversely, the picture might be of the listener as they are (their human condition) or as they might become (the call to holiness). There are other variations on the theme and it is by no means a perfect analogy, but it is a useful one. In some way or another, the preacher hopes that the congregation will leave the church having seen presented to them an image of him who made us or of him who died for us or having a better picture of themselves, standing in the need of grace or standing in robes of righteousness. Louis XIV of France is supposed to have told Jean-Baptiste Massillon, the Bishop of Clermont, 'Whenever I hear you I go away displeased with myself, for I see more of my own character.'[1] Preachers may still be painting portraits that comfort or discomfort their hearers, but the way in which portrait painters have approached their subjects was different in the eighteenth century from earlier periods and is different again today. Congregations listen to sermons as they view portraits, and have expectations about the form that each presentation should have. A difference in sermon form may represent a challenge to or an acknowledgement of a change in expectations.

The purpose of this book is to explore some of those differences and to ask if the techniques in which the homiletic portrait painters of the past were adept have any value for preachers today. It does so by looking at eight periods in history and the

---

1 O. C. Edwards, *A History of Preaching*, vol. 1, Nashville: Abingdon Press, 2004, p. 598.

form that typical preaching has taken in each of those periods. The method employed is selective if not arbitrary, but a study such as this cannot claim to be comprehensive in its treatment either of the history of preaching (there are many excellent works on that) or of the forming of the sermon (on which, again, much material is available). What it can do is to point the reader to a selection of the best of the past and to suggest how that might contribute to the best of the present. That this is no more than a selection from a vast range of material is evident throughout this book, as is the fact that I have been picking up jewels from places where others have mined deeply. This short work can in no way claim to add to the enormous scholarship on which I have been dependent (and of which I have only been able to read a part) on each of the preachers whose work is examined here. Each preacher whose work is approached here has been the subject of meticulous research by experts in the field, and I have to acknowledge my debt to them and to admit my presumption in invading subjects about which I can profess to know so little.

I am grateful to all those who have enabled me to invade in this way and to dip into the enormous amount of material available for a study such as this. In particular, my thanks are due to the staff of St Deiniol's Library and the Cambridge University Library, and to those anonymous and invisible assistants of twenty-first-century research – the online librarians of the various websites I have consulted, in particular 'Fire and Ice' and 'The Newman Reader'. I would also like to record my gratitude to the Methodist Connexion and my own circuit for the privilege of sabbatical leave in the autumn of 2007 when most of the work on this book was undertaken; to Peter Ede who first introduced me to some of the ideas in Chapter 3 and Kenton Anderson who made available his sermon used in Chapter 8; to the congregation at York Central Methodist Church who were unwitting guinea pigs as I tried out some of the ideas in Chapter 4; to my daughter Abigail for her help in producing the Mind Map in Chapter 3; to my son Michael, who assisted with the indexing; and to my wife Lesley, who has borne patiently with me as I have worked on this project.

INTRODUCTION

Matters of Form

'May the words of my mouth, and the meditation of our hearts, be acceptable in your sight, O Lord, our strength and our redeemer.' So, with an adaptation of a verse from Psalm 19, have thousands of preachers begun their sermons over the years. It is a prayer that expresses a pious hope that what has been prepared with prayer and study, and is about to be delivered with varying degrees of confidence, might be fitting as part of the worship of Almighty God.

Mercifully, many would say, we do not find out until Judgement Day what he whose acceptance is craved thinks about the preaching offered in his name. More immediate are the responses of those who listen from below, rather than above, the pulpit. Some responses can be and are offered immediately – through smiles, nods, mutters of 'Amen', or even shouts of 'Alleluia!' – or through fidgeting, sleeping and even leaving the church. Other responses come after further consideration, at the church door or later, from a courteous 'thank you' to a query about a theological nicety. Whether or not the preacher discovers if their preaching was deemed 'acceptable' by those who heard it, the congregants will each make up their own mind on the subject. Opinions may vary from one listener to another and (obviously) about one preacher as opposed to another. Some of those opinions will be about what was said (the content of the sermon): strong reactions can be expressed, for example, if the preacher chooses to articulate a controversial opinion, particularly if the sermon has tackled 'hot issues' relating to the social or political life of the Church or the nation. Some opinions may be about the feelings engendered in the hearers (the effect of the sermon): 'It made me think' is something most preachers will hear at a church door on numerous occasions (though the far rarer 'It made me act' would be infinitely preferable to many preachers). More often, however, what excites most response is the way in which the preacher presented their material (the form or structure of the sermon): 'I found it difficult to follow', 'It wasn't really a sermon', 'It seemed to go round in circles' are some of the common responses from 'dissatisfied customers'.

A common diagnosis offered in the event of such negative response is that the sermon suffered from 'being unstructured'. Listeners expect to hear a discernible form, with a clear message presented in an organized fashion. It is common, when discussing their own or others' sermons, for preachers to talk about this as 'the structure' of the sermon. Since the publication of H. Grady Davis' *Design for Preaching* many homileticians have recognized that 'structure' is a term that implies a mechanical approach to the task, and prefer to speak about the 'form' of a sermon. The central thesis of this book – that form matters – is a concern that has been echoed through centuries of preaching. Boyd Carpenter (in his lectures in the 1890s) put it simply when he maintained that there were three requisites to a sermon – 'order, order, and order'.[1] Less directly, Robert of Basevorn in the fourteenth century expressed his understanding of the preaching task when he opined that 'a thing is formally transmitted and taught when a continuation carries through in an orderly way what the beginning of the work promises or proffers for investigation, and what the end brings to a conclusion

---

1 W. Boyd Carpenter, *Lectures on Preaching*, London & New York, 1895, p. 139.

. . . thus one who deals with the divine word . . . should have an organized method of procedure'.[2]

For sound practical reasons, then, form is important to both the preacher and the congregation, and an effective sermon is one that has been given a form appropriate both to its material and to the capacity of the congregation to receive it. Of course, form is not all, and never could be. The image of the skeleton that gives shape to the body remains a useful (but maybe not a completely adequate) idea in the teaching of preachers;[3] it is the body that needs to be seen, but a body is not a body without a skeleton. A preacher who wants merely to display the way in which the sermon has been shaped (so that the congregation emerges full of admiration for the way in which the hip bone was connected to the thigh bone) may well fail to clothe the bones in flesh (so that no one hears the word of the Lord). But equally (and obviously), a preacher who has a message to proclaim but no way of giving it a beginning, a middle and an end, may not completely fail to communicate (the twentieth-century Methodist W. Edwin Sangster was persuaded that 'sincerity, passion, and the blessing of God can do marvels, even with the formless'),[4] but will fail to communicate all that they intended. Well formed preaching has a framework in which preacher and congregation can with some confidence explore the Word of God together. Poorly formed preaching can lead to anxiety on the part of both the preacher and their hearers.

A local Methodist church recently experimented with the use of Power Point in worship. Instead of being handed hymn books as they came in, the congregants were told that all the words they needed would be displayed on a screen. One of the comments that was made in conversation after the service was that there had been a disconcerting element to the singing because (in order that they might be large enough to be visible) the words

---

2 *The Form of Preaching*, pref. in J. J. Murphy, *Three Rhetorical Arts*, Berkeley and Los Angeles: The University of California Press, 1971, p. 116.

3 *Faith and Worship*, Peterborough: Methodist Publishing House, 2003, p. 32.

4 W. E. Sangster, *The Craft of Sermon Construction*, London: Epworth Press, 1954, p. 63.

were displayed a verse at a time. When an unfamiliar song was presented, there was no indication of its length. Were the people seeing the whole of what they were asked to sing or a quarter of it? Were these words the verse or the chorus? Without being able to see the place of what was immediately before them in the greater whole, some of the congregation felt unnerved. Whether the reasons for this were conscious or subconscious is not clear; the latter is more probable. They may have been practical – how much breath is this going to need? They may have been theological – is this all about God the Son or are there verses about the Father and the Spirit still to be sung? They may have been poetic – are there other stanzas to balance this one? The problem was nothing to do with the content or style of the material – it was simply that the form was not apparent and the worshipping experience was diminished because of that. The same experience can be reported on listening to a sermon. If a worshipper senses, however instinctively, that the point being made is to be balanced by another one, or that the preacher has reached a particular stage in an argument, the message can be heard and understood. A parallel with listening to music is used by both Davis and Mike Graves.[5] A concert goer does not need to have been taught the principles of sonata form to be able to hear how, for example, the first movement of a Mozart symphony presents two main themes, develops one or both, and then recapitulates them. Because the music has been organized in a classical form the listener always has a sense that the notes being heard are contributing to an ordered whole and will have some expectation of where the composer is next going to take his material.

There is a more profound reason why form matters. Dietrich Bonhoeffer expressed this with his understanding that preaching is an expression of the *Sacramentum Verbi*.[6] For Augustine, preaching was 'the daily bread of the faithful'.[7] The Word that

---

5 H. G. Davis, *Design for Preaching*, Philadelphia: Fortress Press, 1958, p. 143; M. Graves, *The Sermon as Symphony*, Valley Forge: Judson Press, 1997, pp. xvff.

6 *Worldly Preaching* quoted in R. Lischer (ed.), *The Company of Preachers*, Grand Rapids, Michigan and Cambridge, UK: Eerdmans, 2002, p. 39.

7 A. D. R. Polman (tr. A. J. Pomerans), *The Word of God in St Augustine*,

became flesh in Bethlehem is the Word that takes form in bread and wine and is the Word that speaks to his people through the reading and exposition of Scriptures in worship. Of course, Sangster was correct – that does sound almost blasphemous,[8] but it is at one with the audacity of believing that the Second Person of the Holy Trinity was born in a stable and died on a gibbet. Audacious also is the belief that Christ who presented himself to us in the form of a servant presents himself in the form of bread and wine. That it is audacious to believe that Christ presents himself to his people in the form of a sermon makes the preacher humble; it also means that the form of the sermon is important because it is a sacred vehicle for the Word of Life. As Calvin argued, the Word is the same Word as is present in the Scriptures, although it comes through the hands of another.[9]

That sacred vehicle can have many forms. It is difficult to think of, or even to imagine, a type of discourse which has appeared in so many different guises while having a continuous history and being recognizably the same thing. It might have been called by different names – an address, a homily, a sermon.[10] It might have had different settings – a great cathedral, a small chapel, a private house – or been associated with a particular purpose – an evangelical outreach, an academic event, a major liturgical occasion. Its length might have varied enormously, from the briefest of reflections to the third turning of the hourglass. Its structure, as this study will show, might have been shaped by factors only tangentially related to the history of the Church. Its quality may have been variable. It would be strange were any of this not so, given the ubiquity of the sermon in the religious practice of men and women over thousands of years. What has been common in the Church is that as the meaning of the story of salvation has been explored by one person sharing his or her thoughts with a

---

Grand Rapids: Eerdmans, 1961, pp. 173f. Augustine's own sermons, however, are notorious for their lack of recognizable structure.

8 Sangster, *op. cit.*, p. 17.

9 T. H. L. Parker, *Calvin's Preaching*, Louisville: Westminster John Knox, 1992, pp. 23f.

10 In this study the terms 'sermon' and 'homily' are treated as approximate synonyms.

congregation, the people have received the Sacramental Word, albeit (through time and place) in very different forms. Or that perhaps they have struggled to receive the Word – because the form in which it was presented was not one in which (to some at least) the Word was recognizable.

Mike Graves identifies what he calls 'Congregational Acoustics'.[11] By this he means that the congregation comes to worship with the anticipation that preaching will be delivered in a particular form or in one of a number of particular forms. The congregant believe that they know what a sermon is and whether what is offered is merely 'an address', 'a talk', or 'a lecture'. Changing the form of what is preached can be more unsettling to a congregation than introducing radical content. Conversely (and this is central to the argument of a homiletician like Graves) changing the form may help to make the Word more acceptable (though not necessarily less unsettling). Telling the story differently can make the story better heard just as those responsible for adapting classic literature for radio, television or cinema will seek to do so in such a way that they enable the audience to hear the story as they themselves have heard it. A number of factors will restrict how this is done. There are the limitations of the medium, the budget, the abilities and wills of the performers, and a host of other concerns that have to be taken into account. There may also be the attitude (or perceived attitude) of the audience. In what form do those who will view or hear this adaptation expect it to be? How far can their expectations be challenged? Can this audience be presented with a story in a way that one of an earlier generation could not or were not?

Among the Sherlock Holmes stories of Sir Arthur Conan Doyle is 'The Blue Carbuncle'.[12] In it we are told of James Ryder who, working at a hotel, stole a precious stone. Panicking, he hid it but lost the hiding place. Both hiding place and jewel turned up, by chance, in Holmes' possession. Ryder had arranged for a plumber with a criminal record, one John Horner, to be framed

---

11 *The Sermon as Symphony*, p. 32.
12 A. Conan Doyle, *The Adventures of Sherlock Holmes*, London: Penguin, 1994, pp. 150–72.

for the theft. Holmes (of course) discovered the true culprit and secured the exoneration of Horner. The story has been dramatized for radio on at least two occasions. In the one, an earlier version, produced by Harry Alan Towers (probably from the 1950s), the story is told much as Conan Doyle wrote it. Horner never appears. In Bert Coules' later version for BBC radio (made in the 1990s), the play begins with Horner and his fiancée in discussion before he is arrested for the burglary. Adapted from the same written text, the two versions are very different. In one, the audience is presented with an interesting problem and its ingenious solution; in the other the audience shares in the anxiety of a man wrongfully arrested. The problem of crime is real in both cases, but it can be seen from different angles. Radio producers clearly felt that the earlier generation either needed or expected a more direct handling of the material.[13]

Whether consciously or not preachers in every generation have had to rise to the challenge to tell the story in such a way that it is better heard. The form of the sermon has changed. What a modern listener 'knows' to be the form that a sermon should have may be very different from what our forebears 'knew' and expected. One obvious example of this in British Methodism (this author's own denomination) is that the form has contracted in the last generation.[14] The half-hour or more for which Sangster or his contemporary and friend Leslie Weatherhead would expect to be able to command his congregation's attention is rarely experienced by their co-religionists today. The tradition (observed now in the breach in most places) that a Methodist chapel should have a copy of John Wesley's *Forty-Four Sermons* to hand in the vestry in case the appointed preacher fail to appear seems extraordinary. How many Methodists are used to a diet of solid biblical exposition and theoretical discussion that addresses two questions which are laid out at the end of the introduction? These immediate observations concern developments within one

---

13 Graves makes similar comments about television programmes and sermon structure in *The Fully Alive Preacher: Recovering from Homiletical Burnout*, Louisville and London: Westminster John Knox, 2006, pp. 107f.

14 This, of course, is not true of all other denominations.

Christian denomination over a comparatively short historical period. Taking an overview of the Church Catholic in two millennia, it is clear that there are many ways in which what was acceptable once might struggle to find acceptance in another age.

In the following chapters, some of those who were deemed by their contemporaries 'most acceptable' over those two millennia are studied. They are not necessarily the most famous preachers of Christian history (though some of them are). They have been chosen because they offer forms of preaching which were in some way characteristic of and in some way a response to the needs of their age. Each chapter attempts, therefore, to place the preacher in context, in terms of the history of preaching, the history of the Church and the wider historical situation. This is not a comprehensive history of the form of the sermon. As far as the author is aware, such a survey is yet to be written. What the present study attempts to do is to pause at a few points in that history, to hear what the preachers were doing, and to analyse how they were doing it. Even within that, some limits have to be acknowledged. Of the hundreds of millions of sermons that have been preached, those which survive on paper are but a tiny fraction and those which have been published for a wider audience a smaller proportion still. To study those in the name of studying preaching is to be restricted to a large but extremely limited field. There are other limitations that have to be recognized. First, the practice of preaching is not exclusively Christian (though, of course, the understanding of it as *sacramentum verbi* is); there are histories of Islamic preaching and of Jewish preaching, but those are not part of the subject of this book. Second, Christian preaching has itself fallen into different categories. The sermons that are studied here are those which have been taken for the most part from liturgical contexts. That is to say that, generally speaking, they were preached (as far as can be established) in a Christian building to (at least nominally) Christian people.[15] In

---

15 Some of the sermons discussed in Chapters 3 and 5 may prove exceptions to this rule.

itself, that situation constitutes part of the demand of a recognizable form. Another study might be offered on the forms of evangelistic preaching, of those sermons which have been preached to those outside the Church intending to draw them into its membership, but that is not to be found in these pages.

There is a further restriction that must be noted. The historical approach here restricts the sermons under consideration to what we might loosely call Christendom; this is preaching as it has been offered since Constantine made Christianity the favoured religion of the Roman Empire. What that means is that, very broadly speaking, all the preachers under consideration here had a common goal. They wanted their congregations to move more deeply into a faith which they purported already to believe. As Benedicta Ward noted of the second of these subjects, the Venerable Bede, the aim was 'to lead to the conversion of life through prayer'.[16] How successfully that goal was achieved by any of the preachers or sermons under discussion here is, of course, impossible to say. How the preachers shaped their material better to achieve that aim is something that can be explored and can possibly, with the same concern, be imitated.

It might be complained that the choice of subjects in this study is somewhat arbitrary. Preaching is offered Sunday by Sunday all over the world, but the later chapters reflect only the British and American situations; while these are likely to be of greatest familiarity to the reader, it has to be admitted that a great deal has been ignored. That certain individual preachers have been made the focus might also be criticized. In some cases, the selection needs no defending. John Chrysostom stands out as a master of preaching, in the opinion of some scholars 'the greatest homiletic preacher of the Greek Church'.[17] The Venerable Bede is one of the very few preachers of the early Middle Ages who has left a significant body of evidence to be considered. Charles Simeon had enormous influence in the early nineteenth

---

16 Benedicta Ward SLG, *The Venerable Bede*, London: Geoffrey Chapman, 1990, p. 43.

17 G. A. Kennedy, *Greek Rhetoric under Christian Emperors*, Princeton: Princeton University Press, 1983, p. 241.

century as did William Edwin Sangster in the late twentieth; the final chapter attempts to offer a representative sample of rapidly developing academic and pastoral work in homiletics. Other examples of Victorian preaching might have been included, but only John Henry Newman offers both Anglican and Catholic practice to be studied. It could be argued that the representative of the later middle ages, William Peyraut, does not stand out as an outstanding theologian or practitioner; he is simply typical of the hundreds of friars who were preaching 'thematic' sermons. Finally, Stephen Charnock is not the most famous of the seventeenth-century Puritans but his sermons have been examined here because of the sheer weight of doctrine that he asks the form to carry.

One of the problems about tackling the Puritan sermon is the question of terminology. To talk about the form (or structure) of a sermon implies an understanding of what a sermon is and how that can be accessed. But a sermon is (by definition) an oral phenomenon. In its truest sense, it exists when it is preached, not when it is printed. In its fullest manifestation, the form of the sermon includes elements which cannot be included on a printed page – the range of the preacher's voice, the pace with which the sermon is delivered, the liturgical and social setting. As Barbara Brown Taylor notes, 'In some cases, a printed sermon is no more than a rumour of what the sermon was really about.'[18] Given that preaching is (again by definition) a time-limited phenomenon, and that a sermon is a time-bound event, it could be argued that analysing the texts of sermons that have been preached is rather like picking over a cadaver *post mortem*. Experience would beg to differ. One of the remarkable features of the sermons discussed in this book is their ability still to speak years if not centuries after they were committed to paper. It might be assumed that the oral event was even more remarkable, although the negative views expressed about, for example, John Wesley's preaching, serve as a reminder that it could mean that

---

18 Barbara Brown Taylor, *The Seeds of Heaven*, 2nd edn, Louisville: Westminster John Knox, 2004, p. viii.

to be present at a sermon may have offered access to less than reading a text.[19]

The relationship between printed sermons and their oral originals (if there were such originals) can be a complex matter. Some preachers (John Henry Newman in his Anglican days is an example) took a full text into the pulpit and delivered what was on the paper, so there can be reasonable confidence that what has been published (for example in *Parochial and Plain Sermons*) is what was heard by the congregation (in the University Church of St Mary the Virgin, Oxford). Other sermons are delivered without the aid of notes, either from the preacher's memory or with a degree of extemporization. That they have survived as texts is due to the preacher writing them up after the event or to a stenographer making a transcript from notes taken during the delivery. The former, apparently, was the practice of Friedrich Schleiermacher, while the other was the way in which preachers as different as John Chrysostom, John Calvin and Charles Haddon Spurgeon saw their sermons reach a wider audience, although it has to be noted that often the drafts were edited by those three preachers before publication. Other sermons (the Church of England's *Book of Homilies* is an obvious example) were probably never preached by those who wrote them, but were written with the intention that they might be read to a congregation by those unauthorized or too modest, busy, lazy or ignorant to produce their own material. In the eighteenth century there was considerable traffic in sermons, with men of letters (such as Laurence Sterne and Samuel Johnson)[20] having profitable sidelines in sermon production. The question therefore arises as to what is and what is not a sermon. Richard Hooker was one of the foremost preachers of his day, but only ten of his 'sermons' have survived and are available in published form. Only three of these can unambiguously be described as sermons.[21] The sermons of Charnock as we have

---

19 O. C. Edwards, *A History of Preaching*, vol. 1, Nashville: Abingdon Press, 2004, p. 414.

20 Edwards, *op. cit.*, vol. 1, p. 444.

21 Philip Secor, *The Sermons of Richard Hooker*, London: SPCK, 2001, p. xiii.

them may even be only the notes of what actually was delivered (which would mean that the sermon itself was much longer than the published version) while the relationship between the texts which John Wesley published (as evidence of his doctrine) and the sermons he preached is far from clear.[22] In many cases, we shall never know whether or not or to what extent the words we have in print represent an oral preaching event. For the purpose of this study it has been assumed, therefore, that the text of the sermon that has been published is as close as the modern student can get to the delivered sermon. Again, the charge that this is arbitrary can be made with some justice.

Yngve Brilioth found that 'the history of preaching is a fascinating field for a purely theoretical study, but it gains its real interest when it is related to the needs of the present time'.[23] This study does not aim to be antiquarian. The forms of the sermons studied here are examined under the microscope with a view to the needs of the contemporary preacher. Are there lessons from the past that can be learned in the twenty-first-century study and put into practice in the twenty-first-century pulpit? The chapter on the modern homileticians answers the question for itself. Sangster's methods still have a considerable following, at least amongst British Methodists, and what he observed (if not what he prescribed) will be familiar to many hearing sermons today. It is with the material of the first six chapters that the issue of contemporary relevance may seem less obvious, so in each of these chapters an experiment has been attempted. A sermon is planned using some of the methods explored in the chapter and connections are made (as sometimes they are earlier in the chapter) between the practice of the past and contemporary approaches and techniques in preaching. Sometimes, and this has been the great delight of this study, those connections are surprising.

---

22 Edwards, *op. cit.*, vol. 1, p. 440.
23 *Landmarks in the History of Preaching*, London: SPCK, 1950, p. 39.

AGAINST HERODIAS

The Preaching of John Chrysostom

Broadly speaking, from 500 years before the birth of Christ to 500 years after that event, the story of Europe was the story of Rome. Rome's rise from being little more than a collection of villages in central Italy, through its unrivalled dominance of the known world, to the beginnings of its retreat to become a constantly threatened fortress state on the Mediterranean's eastern seaboard, is the backdrop against which most history of that period needs to be understood. During that millennium, again broadly speaking, Rome experienced three major periods of political upheaval, each of which heralded a new phase in the story of Roman power and a new phase in the religious story of Rome.

The first of these upheavals is shrouded in legend. In about the year 509 BC, the Romans expelled their king, Tarquin Superbus. Tarquin was believed to be the last of seven monarchs who had ruled what had been no more than a city state. In the late sixth century BC, one Servius Tullius had given the city a political organization which was refined in a series of political manoeuvrings and wars that followed the end of the monarchy, from which Rome emerged as a proud independent republic with a system of government by senate and consuls that was to last for 400 years.

The city also appears to have acquired from this period a distinctive national religious system, adapted from the pantheons of their Italian and Greek neighbours. The Roman Republic was always understood to be a religious as well as a political entity in which the *Pontifex Maximus* was an important figure and the deliberations of the Senate and the processes of democracy were regarded as sacred events. Belief in the pantheon that the state promoted was part of a nexus of thinking; to the twenty-first-century mind this was a largely superstitious faith system, which included the searching of auguries before any political or military action, the offering of sacrifice in the hope of a propitious outcome to any expedition and the belief that certain individuals could claim their descent from the gods.

The second upheaval is far better documented and far better known. During the mid-first century BC, Rome suffered a series of civil wars, as first Julius Caesar and Mark Antony defeated Pompey, Cato, and Scipio, then Antony and Caesar's heir Octavian defeated Brutus and Cassius, and finally (in 31–30 BC) Octavian defeated Antony (and Cleopatra). The victorious Octavian styled himself Augustus, and the Roman Republic gave way to the Empire (in effect a military dictatorship). Octavian's considerable political acumen, the gradual way in which he imposed the change on Rome (so much so that historians disagree about when his reign as emperor can be reckoned properly to begin),[1] and his longevity (he lived until AD 14) ensured that there was no return to the republican system after his death. Even during the difficult years of weak emperors and political instability (such as that which followed the death of Nero in AD 68) there was apparently no significant desire to abolish the imperial office. Like the Republic, the Empire had religious as well as political dimensions. The emperor was usually *Pontifex Maximus,* and it became increasingly common for an emperor to proclaim his predecessors (or even, in Caligula's case, himself) divine. To be irreligious therefore was to undermine the institutions of the state.

---

1 M. Le Glay et al. (tr. A. Nevill), *A History of Rome*, 2nd edn, Oxford: Blackwell, 2001, p. 169.

It was in the wake of this second seismic shift that Christianity came into being and, despite the obvious danger that the demands of conformity to the official cult posed for Christians, the early decades of the Empire proved to be a propitious time for a new religion to be born. The evangelizing missions of Paul and others were facilitated by the peace which Augustus had imposed on the Mediterranean and the communications network that was being developed. From at least the time of Melito of Sardis (whose writings date from the mid-second century AD), and arguably from Luke in the New Testament, Christian apologists noticed that the 'golden age of Augustus' accompanied the early years of the Church, and that the interests of the Church and those of the Empire (*pace* the writer of the book of Revelation) coincided. 'It was for the good that our doctrine flourished alongside the Empire in its happy inception . . . from the time of the principate of Augustus no evil has befallen it.'[2]

The third major change in the story of Rome came late in the third century AD. Octavian's empire had become an unwieldy administrative structure. That no emperor had managed to rule it without major difficulty throughout the century was not entirely due to the poor quality of those whom the army installed (although that was part of the problem). There was urgent need for reform and this was recognized by Diocletian, who became emperor in 284. Diocletian's solution was to divide the Empire into two and to propose that each half be ruled by a senior and a junior emperor (an Augustus and a Caesar). Part of the plan was that the Augusti would retire at the same time and be succeeded by their Caesars, thus ensuring an orderly transition of power and an end to the frequent civil wars. It was an idealistic programme, and one which unsurprisingly did not survive the untimely death of one of the co-emperors (Constantius) or the end of Diocletian's own personal rule. From the series of conflicts which followed his abdication in 305, a sole emperor was to emerge triumphant – Constantine I. But fundamental parts of Diocletian's reform were to survive; the division of the Empire

---

2 Melito of Sardis in Eusebius, *Ecclesiastical History*, IV, 26 (tr. G. A. Williamson, *The History of the Church*, Harmondsworth: Penguin, 1965, pp. 187f.)

into east and west was an enduring feature, and the shift of power from Rome to a new capital (which Constantine modestly named Constantinople) was to shape the future of the Empire for the rest of its existence (which, as Byzantium, was until 1453). Once again, the nature of the institution changed. The Roman Empire was now a police state; Diocletian and his successors maintained their increasingly exalted position through a network of spies and informers and by the rapid and brutal oppression of any putative insurgency.

Just as Rome's pagan pantheon had emerged from the upheavals around the year 500 BC, and the birth of Christianity had occurred (and an imperial cult developed) in the wake of Octavian's triumph, so a new phase in the religious life of the Empire began with the victories of Constantine. In 312, at the battle of the Milvian Bridge, he declared himself a Christian. The Church, which under Diocletian and Galerius (his Caesar and successor) had been subject to vicious persecution, was now the favoured religion of the imperial court. As Eusebius expressed it: 'For us who had fixed our hopes on the Christ of God there was unspeakable happiness, and a divine joy blossomed in all hearts as we saw that every place which a little while before had been reduced to dust by the tyrants' wickedness was now, as if from a prolonged and deadly stranglehold, coming back to life.'[3] The transformation in the fortunes of the Church was as complete as it was unexpected. Before Constantine, Christians had seen their buildings closed, the accoutrements of worship confiscated, and their fellow believers martyred. Now they received all the benefits of imperial favour; the construction of new churches was financed from the public purse, Christian leaders were welcomed to high office and laws favourable to the ethics of the emperor's new faith were enacted. Within 70 years of the end of the great persecution instituted by Diocletian, Christianity had become the only official religion of the Empire, and those of other faiths (or of dissident Christian bodies) found themselves subject to punitive measures.

---

3 *Ecclesiastical History* X. 2 (*op. cit.*, p. 382).

Among those who have studied the history of the Church, opinion remains divided on the sincerity and the felicity of Constantine's conversion. Some maintain that it was a cynical ploy by a man whose despotic conduct (which included the murder of his wife and son) over the following 25 years was typical of a tyrant (and anything but Christian) and that his notorious deathbed baptism was the earliest moment at which he can be said to have identified himself with the Church. On that understanding, Constantine's profession of faith was a strategic and Machiavellian manoeuvre designed to gain him support. This seems an unlikely calculation; it is hard to see any political gain for Constantine in embracing a faith which, although it had been steadily growing in influence, was still followed by only a small minority of the Empire's population (possibly about three or four per cent),[4] was badly divided, and counted few of the leading citizens and (crucially) few in the army among its adherents. Whatever his motivation, whether or not Constantine's embracing Christianity was to the benefit of the Church also remains a contentious issue. Those who lament the day that Constantine made the chi-rho his symbol ('there never was a time wherein Satan gained so fatal an advantage over the Church of Christ' according to John Wesley)[5] do so because they believe that it led to imperial interference in the Church and to the Church's becoming identified with the means of power and wealth, thereby sacrificing its earlier purity. Few at the time would have seen it like that. To Constantine's contemporaries it seems all too apparent that the benefits for Christianity far outweighed any disadvantages which followed the emperor's conversion. Even if, as has been argued,[6] the Church had been growing exponentially for 250 years, it is hard to imagine that the rate of expansion could have continued (and accelerated) as it did in the fourth and fifth

---

4 Gibbon reckoned that it could have been five per cent, but Robin Lane Fox argues for a much lower number, estimating that in the mid-third century only two per cent of the empire's population was Christian (*Pagans and Christians*, London: Viking, 1986, pp. 268, 287).

5 Sermon 66. *Works*, 3rd edn, London, 1872, vol. 6, p. 346

6 D. James, *Romans and Christians*, Stroud and Charleston: Tempus, 2002, p. 53.

centuries had Christians continued to be subject to vicious persecution or had the laws which Constantine issued at the prompting of his bishops not been introduced.

That the Christianization of the Roman Empire meant to some degree the imperialization of the faith cannot be denied. Although Constantine was invited to intervene in the North African controversy over Donatism early in his reign, it was his involvement in the Arian controversy that marked a new phase of relations between Church and emperor. His calling of the Council of Nicaea, his commitment to ensuring the effectiveness of its decisions by exiling the opposition, his later hesitations and his sons' Arianizing policies all contributed to 'the orthodox interpretation' of Christian faith being that which was determined by the party who could convince the emperor or his closest advisers of their own position. It was a situation which reached its climax and solution in the Nicene policy of Theodosius I under whose rule the Council of Constantinople brought to an end the Arian controversy.

It was Theodosius who decreed that Roman paganism no longer had a place in the Empire. Constantine's initial moves to favour Christianity had been those of toleration and favouritism; this policy had proven so effective that by the time his nephew Julian (emperor in 360–61) reverted to paganism (partly out of sheer dislike of Constantine and his family), there were Christians in most high places. Even if the Apostate had reigned much longer than the 21 months he occupied the throne, it appears unlikely that he could have succeeded (as he hoped) in eradicating the faith from among the ruling and influential classes. Seventeen years after Julian's death and only 70 after Constantine's conversion, Theodosius outlawed all pagan religious practice. But so rapid a transformation of the fortunes of the old religion would not have changed people's beliefs or customs. Christianity was to remain a largely urban religion for some time,[7] and pagan rhetors operated openly for many years after the Theodosian decrees. But at a less obvious level, fourth- and fifth-

---

7 There was some rural Christian presence, partly as a result of the persecutions of the third century. See Fox, *op. cit.*, p. 287.

century Roman society may have seen not so much the defeat of an ancient way of thinking as its syncretistic merging with the newly popular faith. If the Empire had reconciled itself to Christianity, Christianity had also moved towards the Empire.

Part of the issue here is that Christianity and Roman paganism were not mirror images of each other. Pagan religion (the cultic system of sacrifices, auguries and myths) was separate in the Roman mind from pagan virtue (the encouragement of qualities such as courage and loyalty). Christians have always maintained (theoretically at least) that orthodoxy and orthopraxis are one; Christian trees are known by Christian fruits. As the Church grew numerically in the third century, some of the absolutism of earlier times was abandoned. An example is the growing willingness of Christians to serve in the military,[8] which ironically was where the Great Persecution began.[9] With the conversion of Constantine, the Church began to find itself a major element in a society which had been shaped to a large degree by the paganism of its past. The emperor's policy of building a new city with no pagan temple in it was in some ways a recognition of the incompatibility of his new faith with the old ways of doing things; some of Constantine's political acts (such as his acceptance of the title *Pontifex Maximus*) demonstrated that Christianity had to live with the relics of paganism.

It also had to live with the political reality of imperial power and, for those in the higher echelons of the Church's hierarchy, to live in close proximity to that reality. The fourth century saw a transformation of the role of the bishop; no longer was he the figurehead of opposition to Rome (as, for example, Ignatius of Antioch or Cyprian of Carthage had been). Now, to a greater or lesser extent depending on the distance of his diocese from the capital, his was an appointment that the emperor had to approve (if not to make). So a Christian preacher found himself in an interesting position.[10] The preacher of the third century had been

---

8 Fox, *op. cit.*, p. 304; Helgeland et al., *Christians and the Military*, London: SCM Press, 1987, p. 91.

9 Eusebius, *Ecclesiastical History*, VIII. 4 (*op. cit.*, p. 332).

10 Whatever may have been the case in earlier times, by the early fourth century it appears that all Christian preachers were men.

addressing a gathering of those who might at any stage be asked to surrender their faith or their lives and of whom, therefore, it was safe to assume both a considerable commitment to the faith and no close association with government policy, but the preacher of the fourth century, particularly in cities closely associated with imperial power (such as Constantinople and Milan), would face a congregation that included those who attended for a variety of religious and social reasons, some of whom made no pretence of Christian belief and some of whom were members of the government. So it was that Ambrose (339–97), exercising his episcopal ministry in Milan, could count amongst his listeners the unconverted Augustine (who attended to study the preacher's rhetoric)[11] and, if not always the emperor himself, those from the imperial court who would be sure to report back his denunciations of ecclesiastical policy. The danger was different but, for the preacher unafraid to express his beliefs, no less real than it had been before the rise of Constantine. It is in this context that the ministry of John Chrysostom has to be understood.

John's career is a landmark in the history of preaching. He is the first saint to be remembered primarily as a preacher; his cognomen means 'golden-mouthed'. In his own lifetime, both his fame and his misfortunes can be attributed to the power of his preaching; such was the popularity that he achieved through his homilies, he became the centre of a personality cult and on more than one occasion his removal from one place to another was conducted under cover of darkness for fear that rioting would ensue when it was discovered that he was gone. Whilst the latter part of John's life is well documented (thanks to his own voluminous correspondence, the evidence of his homilies and other writings, and the histories of Sozomen and Socrates), for his earlier years we have much less evidence. Born *c.* 349, he was a native of Antioch and the son of moderately well-to-do parents. His mother was widowed when he was very young, but still contrived to ensure that her son received a good education. He studied with a famous pagan philosopher, Libanius, before, at the age of 18 or 20, entering

---

11 Augustine, *Confessions*, V (tr. E. B. Pusey, *Confessions of Saint Augustine*, London: Nelson, 1938, p. 101).

the service of Melitius, the bishop of Antioch. In 371, he was ordained reader, but resisted further elevation to the priesthood.

The mid-fourth century was a period of confusion and ecclesiastical wrangling as Arian and Nicene Christians both attempted to establish their understanding of the Trinity as the faith of the Church. In 371, Melitius was in exile, expelled from the city by the Arian emperor, Valens. For most of the time of the bishop's banishment, John absented himself from Antioch, becoming an ascetic with the monks on Mt Silpios. After four years of community living, he sought a greater solitude and lived in isolation for two years, submitting himself to a regime of rigorous asceticism which was to have a long-term detrimental effect on his health. With nothing to distract him, John was able to give himself over to the study of the Scriptures, and by the time he returned to Antioch he had learned the whole of the Old and New Testaments by heart. The death of Valens in 378 was followed by the restoration of Melitius to Antioch, and the return of John to serve as his reader. In 381, John was made a deacon (an office which apparently did not at that time include a licence to preach);[12] only in 386 was he finally ordained presbyter by Melitius' successor, Flavian.

Preaching was John's main responsibility as a presbyter. It appears that he was appointed by Flavian to give the homily at services on a regular basis. These would not only be Sunday masses or holy days; series of John's sermons survive which indicate that at certain times of the year (Lent being the prime example) the faithful were expected to attend worship and to hear a homily every day. John appears to have attained an almost instant popularity as a preacher. When he acquired his complimentary cognomen is not clear, but from early in his career he exhibited an ability to please a congregation. In part, this may have been the manner of his delivery; in part it seems to have been due to his rare ability to make the finer points of Christian doctrine (as in his sermons against the Anomoeans) comprehensible to those less educated than he was. His popularity seems to

---

12 J. N. D. Kelly, *Golden Mouth*, Ithaca NY: Cornell University Press, 1995, p. 39.

have brought him fame beyond the membership of the church, as there is evidence that pagans were among his congregation during Lent 387.[13]

In 398, John was appointed bishop of Constantinople, largely through the machinations of the chief eunuch at the imperial court, Eutropius. It was not the election that the bishop of Alexandria, Theophilus, had wanted, and it is no coincidence that John's career came to its unfortunate end largely through the activities of Theophilus. In the imperial capital, John maintained his popularity as a preacher, but was eventually undone by his forthright comments on the activities of the royal household and the authoritarian way in which he ruled his diocese. When Theophilus, summoned to the city to explain his conduct in relation to a group of monks he had excommunicated, so manipulated the situation that he sat in judgement on John rather than *vice versa*, the emperor was persuaded to accept the decrees of the Synod and expel the popular preacher. A brief return did not see (as John had hoped) the quashing of the Synod's verdict, largely because of his unfortunate comparison of the empress to Herodias.[14] Exiled in Armenia, John conducted a vigorous (and successful) campaign to involve the pope in his cause; realizing that John was able to communicate with his supporters too easily, the emperor banished him further to the Black Sea coast, but illness and the ill-treatment he endured at the hands of his guards caused the bishop's death on the journey in 407.

Many of Chrysostom's sermons have survived, more than of any other of the Church Fathers.[15] Like his western contemporary, Ambrose, Chrysostom's status both in his own day and in subsequent periods depended on his preaching. For ecclesiastical historians, this marks something of a new departure with a welcome surfeit of material. Of earlier theologians, the only significant surviving legacy of homiletic material comes from Origen

---

13 Kelly, *op. cit.*, p. 82.
14 Kelly, *op. cit.*, p. 240.
15 R. C. Hill, *Homilies on Genesis (The Fathers of the Church, vol. 74)*, Washington DC: Catholic University of America Press, 1990, p. 3.

(*c*. 185–255) and that, thanks to his condemnation by Justinian, is severely depleted.

In discussing his work (and the work of others) we meet a question of terminology, the detail of which exercises those scholars who specialize in Chrysostom but can be sidestepped here. For the purpose of this study, the terms 'sermon' and 'homily' are used interchangeably. Whether or not Chrysostom or his stenographers viewed them (or their Greek equivalents *logos* and *homelia*) as synonymous is a matter of debate,[16] but there is no clear distinction in structure between the two. Another confusion is that the expository homilies are sometimes referred to as commentaries and it appears that in some cases some of the homiletic features were removed, either by John or an editor, prior to publication. There are also homilies which some scholars maintain were written by John but never preached by him, although some of the particular instances cited have references that could only have come from the liturgical context (such as the moment when John tells his congregation to pay attention to him rather than to the servant lighting the lamps).[17] One of the reasons for the uneven quality of the extant work is the method of production. Whether or not it was John's practice normally to preach without any notes (the ecclesiastical historian Sozomen records one occasion when he preached entirely extemporaneously),[18] it seems clear that his sermons were designed to be delivered orally but were recorded for publication by stenographers and revised by John.[19] Some of them may not have been subject to the author's editing prior to publication and therefore appear far less polished than others.[20]

Not only do the homilies differ in quality, they differ in form. John's orations can be classified in two groups. The first group

16 Hill, *op. cit.*, pp. 6f.

17 W. Mayer and P. Allen, *John Chrysostom*, London and New York: Routledge, 2000, p. 30.

18 Sozomen, *Ecclesiastical History* VIII, 18 (tr. C. D. Hartranft, ed. P. Schaff, *Nicene and Post-Nicene Fathers*, Series 2, vol. 2), p. 889.

19 J. L. Maxwell, *Christianization and Communication in Late Antiquity*, Cambridge: Cambridge University Press, 2006, pp. 6f.

20 *Homilies on Galatians etc.* (ed. P. Schaff, *Nicene and Post-Nicene Fathers*, Series 1, vol. 13), p. 4.

consists of expository sermons. It appears that from at least the time of Origen it was customary for the daily prayer of the church to include a sermon of up to an hour's duration and that that sermon would offer a verse-by-verse exegesis of the biblical passage that had been read.[21] The passage was determined by the *lectio continua* method; the congregation attending every day would hear a book of the Bible read in sequence with both reader and preacher resuming at the point on which they had ended the previous day. This form of sermon seems to have been typical of the early Church and to have survived up to and beyond the Reformation. H. O. Old's belief that it was one of the methods of preaching which the early Church inherited from the Synagogue seems entirely reasonable,[22] although the lack of evidence means that it is impossible to be certain that it was widely used prior to the time of Origen. By Chrysostom's day the form must have been familiar to the congregation; it merits no explanation. To a modern reader it appears to be a somewhat *ad hoc* way of treating the Scripture, as the preacher might comment on only part of a story before breaking until the next service. Sometimes with Chrysostom the divisions are not where they might be expected (partly, of course, because the verse and chapter organization in modern Bibles was a mediaeval invention) and the length of the passage treated can be most uneven. John's homily 48 on Matthew, for example, addresses the story of Jesus' preaching in his home town as well as the narrative of the beheading of John the Baptist, whereas earlier in the series John had devoted three sermons to the opening genealogy and two to the visit of the Magi. In the homilies on Genesis, he concentrated in the first 17 of a series of 67 on what are now the first two chapters, so the pace in dealing with the rest of the book appears (of necessity) to be considerably quicker.

Although it is possible to speak about many of John's homilies as exegesis or commentary on a biblical passage, his contemporary, Julian of Eclanum, noted that there was as much

---

21 H. O. Old, *The Reading and Preaching of the Scriptures*, vol. 1, Grand Rapids: Wm Eerdmans, 1998, p. 329.

22 Old, *op. cit.*, vol. 1, pp. 102f.

exhortation as exposition.[23] Typically, John's method was to work through the verses of his passage, offering explanatory comments. These are sometimes enlarging on the historical or literal meaning of the text. It is a generalization, but a fair one, to note that Antiochene theologians tended to focus on literal meanings rather than to develop any allegorical interpretation. The alternative to a literal reading in Antiochene thinking was an ethical one, and John would often draw from a text a moral lesson for the congregation. When the passage had been explored line by line in this way, John would usually expand on the final point or on the summary of the whole text with moral injunctions for the congregation, before ending with a final benediction or doxology.

An example of this method could be taken from almost anywhere in the collection of homilies. Homily 64 on Matthew resumes the series at chapter 19 verse 27.[24] There is no introduction and no attempt to remind the congregation of what they heard on the previous occasion. John picks up on the comment of Peter that the disciples have left everything to follow Jesus. He asks what this everything is that the disciples have left and connects Peter's question to Jesus' reply to the rich young ruler, arguing that the disciples had made themselves poor in order to follow Jesus.

The next verse gives John a historical problem; Jesus promises that the disciples will sit on 12 thrones, but one of the 12 disciples is Judas. This leads John to a discussion of the principles of Old Testament prophecy. A punishment promised by God could be averted by the repentance of those threatened, whereas a prophesied blessing could be forfeited by a fall from grace. That, John concluded, was to be the fate of Judas. He moves on to the next verse in which Jesus talks of anyone who had left possessions or family for his sake being rewarded; the comments of Jesus, therefore, do not only refer to the twelve.

---

23 Hill, *op. cit.*, p. 11.
24 P. Schaff (ed.), *The Nicene and Post-Nicene Fathers, Series 1*, vol. 10, p. 821.

But John is not yet ready to move on in the text. He pauses to discuss the statement about judging the 12 tribes of Israel. He refers his congregation back to Matthew 12.41f., in which Jesus had prophesied that the people of Nineveh and the Queen of the South would condemn Israel. The judging, therefore, is not the focus of the promise in this instance; the reward for the disciples is the honour accorded them by having thrones with Christ. But John notices that in these words it is implied that the disciples will have to suffer with Jesus before they share his glory. John finds that the next verse strikes a different note. 'Many who are first will be last and the last first' refers, John says, both to the disciples and to righteous Jews. His implication seems to be that positions in the kingdom should never be taken for granted, but John does not dwell on this. He moves swiftly to the next section.

The remainder of the passage is the parable of the workers in the vineyard. John does not work through this verse by verse but discusses it as a unit. This is John's usual approach to such material: 'as I am always saying, the parables must not be explained throughout word for word, since many absurdities will follow.'[25] When he comes to ask what this parable means, John's initial problem is the saying with which it ends, the repeating of 'the last will be first . . .' That is not what happens in the parable, John argues. There, all are treated equally. In order to wrestle with this, he offers a brief allegorical interpretation of the setting and then suggests that the problem might be the sinful envy of those called first. The point of the parable was to urge those conscious of their calling to be earnest in the pursuit of virtue. John then asks why the characters in the story were called at different times, and argues that they were not, some simply responded later than the others. John's text differs from most modern translations, and he also finds himself discussing the additional words, 'many are called but few chosen'. All this, it seems to him, refers to those who have forfeited the blessings that were offered, both the Jews (whom John often has in view) and lapsed Christians.

---

25 *Hom. Matt.* 47, 1 (*op. cit.*, p. 616).

The remainder of the sermon is an entreaty to the congregation to live lives worthy of their calling. Free from commenting on the text, John offers a wide-ranging analysis of what it means to be a Christian. He builds up a picture to show how high the standard of the kingdom is. Then he offers positive examples of those who had lived virtuously and given generously (bestowing of alms on the poor was always a favourite theme of John's and something that he was repeatedly urging his congregants to do) and argues that the only way to do this is to take Jesus himself as the model. Again he counselled against envy and concludes that the congregation should be examining their own conduct in order to be prepared for the judgement of Christ. The sermon ends with a doxology.

A very different approach is evident in some of John's other homilies. Because of a particular event or occasion, John would sometimes preach a sermon which bore no relation to a particular biblical text but addressed a subject. His model here would be drawn from the practice of classical rhetoric which, of course, he had learned from Libanius. Early in his career (with an episode which may be the initial reason for his fame as a preacher), John found that this sort of preaching was required of him. In 387, a new and unpopular tax was imposed on the city of Antioch. Rioting broke out in the city in the course of which the statues of the emperor (Theodosius) and his late wife were destroyed. The Christianization of the Empire had not been so far developed as to cause those conscious of the imperial dignity to 'turn the other cheek' in response to such an insult. The furious Theodosius' first response was to order the execution not only of the rioters but also of the city officers and the destruction of the city. Flavian, the bishop, travelled to Constantinople in order to plead for the people, and a special imperial investigation was launched. Eventually, clemency was shown; the city lost some of its status, but all who might have been held responsible (apart from the rioters themselves) were pardoned.[26] These events dominated the Lent of that year, when John (it appears) was appointed to preach at the daily office. A series of 21 homilies survives; in them the

---

26 Kelly, *op. cit.*, pp. 72–9.

preacher responds to the fears of the citizens as well as exhorting them to Lenten penance and the amendment of life. In particular, John was concerned about the swearing of oaths, a practice which, he maintained, had become so widespread that the anger of God had been incurred against Antioch.

Having secured the renewal of the emperor's good favour, Flavian returned to Antioch for Easter; the last of the homilies celebrates his return and the Paschal feast. In that homily, John was extravagant in his praise of the bishop. He had been equally fulsome in the sermon that followed the bishop's departure. This homily, the third of the series, offers a model for the use of classical forms of rhetoric. John had two aims. One was to comfort an anxious people, since the fear of imperial reprisals was real and appears to have led to an increase in John's congregation as worried citizens rushed to prayer;[27] the other was to remind Christians of their Lenten obligations. John relates the two in this address, the pattern of which can be described as Introduction (or exordium), Narration, Confirmation, Exhortation and Peroration, a standard model of classical rhetoric.

The purpose of the Introduction in classical rhetoric was to establish the relationship between the speaker and the auditory. This John does by lamenting the absence of Flavian, whom he praises as the good shepherd who has gone to lay down his life for the sheep. The mission is important because of the status of Antioch as 'the head and mother of all that lie towards the East'. The Narration, that part of the speech which laid out the issue at the heart of the oration, follows; John paints a picture of how, by his eloquence and his manifest sanctity, Flavian would appeal to the emperor's clemency. The mission, John is sure, will be successful, not only because Theodosius is humane and Flavian is pious, but because God himself will guide the bishop's pleading and the ruler's response. The duty of those who watch and wait is to support the mission with prayer.

The Confirmation would traditionally be the point when a speaker supported the argument with evidence. John does this first by reference to the example of Esther, who had to go before

---

27 Kelly, *op. cit.*, p. 76.

the Persian ruler on behalf of her people. He then argues that the time of year (Lent) is right for fervent and effective prayer to be offered and reminds the people of the duties of abstinence. But the proper abstinence is not from the prohibited foods but from sinful behaviour and John draws attention to the response of the people of Nineveh to the preaching of Jonah.

This leads John into the fuller part of the Exhortation. He has particular sins in mind from which he urges the people to desist and he cautions them especially against slander. He expounds the ways in which it is wrong to insult another person, a catalogue which brings him back to the concern foremost in his audience's mind, the insult to the emperor. The current troubles should be a lesson to them, he says, and make them aware of their lack of respect for God. He is confident that the immediate danger will soon pass and that the mercy of the emperor will be sought successfully, but he worries lest the Antiochenes remain in their sinful behaviour towards God. He warns against assuming that if Antioch is spared it shows that no judgement is due to it; the guilty sometimes escape human justice but never that of God, and the example of Joseph's brothers is used to demonstrate that the consequence of sins can be recognized years after the event.

The Peroration urges the Antiochenes to take seriously the keeping of Lent. Three things in particular should be corrected – speaking ill of others, bearing enmity and swearing oaths (a theme to which he will return many times in later homilies). If they can change their ways, he is confident not only that 'there will be deliverance from the present calamity' but also of their eternal reward, an assertion with which John reaches his closing doxology.

Libanius, John's (pagan) teacher, is supposed to have been asked by his pupils whom he would like to succeed him as the master of his school and to have replied, 'John, had not the Christians stolen him from us.'[28] It is clear that a major reason for John's popularity (and for the animosity that he could pro-voke which led to his downfall) was his oratorical ability. The homilies on the statues demonstrate that he was able to harness

---

28 Edwards, *op. cit.*, vol. 1, p. 73.

that in the service of pastoral theology. As always, the text that we have inherited cannot do full justice to these great rhetorical gifts. It is clear that he was an impassioned performer, well aware (apparently from early in his ordained ministry) of his own ability; he was also a well schooled speaker who understood and could use with ease and flexibility the conventions of the day. What is also clear is that (thanks, no doubt, to Libanius' training) he understood the importance of form in his sermons. Whether that form is determined by the nature of the text on which he is preaching (as in many of the homilies that appear in series on biblical books), by a particular occasion (such as those on the feasts of dedication)[29] or (as in some cases) a combination of the two, it is clear that his gifts as a speaker were aided by the limpidity of thought which emerges from the clear organization of his material. His tragedy stemmed from the fact that for one who had the emperor and empress close at hand he sometimes said things all too clearly.

The Chrysostom sermons which combine a particular occasion with the treatment of a biblical text which was addressed in sequence are few in number, but they may well provide a helpful model for the preacher of today. The influential contemporary homiletician Eugene Lowry is reported to have said that if he had been told at the beginning of his ministry 'that United Methodists would one day embrace the use of the lectionary, he would have declared [the speaker] crazy'.[30] The American experience has echoes in Britain also, where amongst the Free Churches preaching on the lectionary became far more common and in some places the norm in the last quarter of the twentieth century. The ecumenical consensus around the Revised Common Lectionary is seen as one of a number of benefits to many churches following the same course of readings. Those who argue in favour of the development point to the consistency of approach that it will give to a church, particularly a church which welcomes different preachers each week. Studies have shown that (contrary perhaps

---

29 E.g. Mayer and Allen, *op. cit.*, pp. 93–7.

30 M. Graves, *The Fully Alive Preacher: Recovering from Homiletical Burn-out*, Louisville and London: Westminster John Knox, 2006, p. 57.

to initial expectation) lectionary preaching causes a wider range of readings to be heard than is the case when the choice of lesson is in the hands of the preacher.[31] Preachers benefit from the enormous range of resources, both in print and online, which are now available to support their ministry, as the lectionary becomes a focus for the exchange of ideas.

There remain, however, those in the Free Churches (and some in other denominations) who are hesitant about the lectionary, claiming that it restricts both the preacher and the local congregation. Tying a preacher to a text (or group of texts) on which they would not otherwise have been drawn to preach restricts the preacher's charism; presenting a set text (or group of texts) to a congregation makes no allowance for local pastoral need. Sometimes, those who take this view argue, a particular situation must be allowed to take precedence. Mike Graves cites 11 September 2001 as an example. In the wake of the attack on the Twin Towers he struggled with a church secretary who discouraged him from abandoning the lectionary.[32] There will be times when a preacher is faced with such a dilemma, but it is possible to argue that in moments like that the lectionary provides an important pastoral answer; despite whatever it is that has happened to shock preacher, congregation, or both, they can turn to the appointed point in the whole Church's rehearsal of the story of salvation and hear God say 'nevertheless . . .'[33]

Chrysostom may provide an answer to this dilemma. Some homilies clearly tackle a particular issue (such as those on the statues or the ones preached at the tombs of the martyrs) and others offer verse-by-verse exegesis (such as most of those on the Pauline epistles), but there are occasions on which he combines both approaches. This was the case in the series on Genesis which

---

31 S. E. Cochran, 'The Christian Year and the Revised Common Lectionary: Helps and Hindrances to Worship Planners and Preachers', in D. M. Greenhaw and R. J. Allen (eds), *Preaching in the Context of Worship*, St Louis: Chalice Press, 2000, p. 63.

32 Graves, *op. cit.*, p. 58.

33 Marva Dawn (quoting Leander Keck), *Reaching Out without Dumbing Down: A Theology of Worship for This Urgent Time*, Grand Rapids, Michigan and Cambridge UK: Wm Eerdmans, 1995, p. 93.

appears to come from the early years of his presbyteral ministry in Antioch.[34] While the form is not invariable, these sermons are often in three parts with an introduction, a central exposition, and a closing exhortation. Sometimes, as Old notes, the three parts are only loosely connected,[35] but connected in some way they are. The most famous and obvious example is the sixth sermon. John had been proceeding at a leisurely pace through the first chapter of the book and had reached the events of the fourth day. But he begins the sermon with a confession of his despair and anger, claiming to be so upset that he is hesitant to preach. The reason for this reticence is that members of the congregation have been to the horse races. Whether John believed the racetrack to be evil *per se* (perhaps remembering that the games had been part of a pre-Christian culture with pagan religious associations) or was simply indignant at the open flouting of Lenten discipline is not clear. What is clear is how strongly he feels on the subject; he compares the Antiochenes to a merchant who has lost everything in a storm, so callously have they thrown away their spiritual wealth. More, he is concerned that some do not appear to be penitent. However, as their father in Christ, it is still his duty to feed them, and so he returns to his study of Genesis.

The middle section of the sermon explores the account of the fourth day of creation. John's central argument, as in most of the early sermons in this series, is that the creative power of God is stressed by the writer of Genesis. This is to challenge any who doubt or who are drawn to worship the creation rather than its Creator. The particular emphasis on the fourth day that John notes is the way in which created things (in this case the celestial bodies) were designed for the benefit of human beings. He brings this section to a close with his comments on the words which are repeated in each part of the creation narrative, 'God saw that it was good. Evening came and morning came . . .'. These are designed, John argues, 'to rivet the sacred truths in our mind'[36]

John then makes the transition to the third (and shortest) sec-

34 Hill, *op. cit.*, p. 8.
35 Old, *op. cit.*, vol. 2, p. 174.
36 *Hom. Gen.*, 6, 19.

tion of the homily by asking the congregation to take all he has said to heart. They are to worship the Creator, not the creation. They worship him best by living lives that are pleasing to him, avoiding relapsing into sin, and therefore not going to the races. With a few more words urging the congregation to find something of greater spiritual benefit to occupy their time, he moves to his final doxology.

A similar method could be employed by a modern preacher who faces a moment of crisis or is aware of an issue that has to be addressed while intending at the same time to remain loyal to an appointed lectionary. The Boxing Day tsunami of 2004 might have provided an example of this. Christians in Britain (as elsewhere) were horrified by the news that dozens of communities in southern Asia had been devastated and thousands of people lost their lives as the sea simply swept away all that was in its path. Over the week that followed the first media reports, the scale of the catastrophe became clear and the shock was enormous. What was bewildering was partly that the ocean alongside which people had lived for generations and from which many had got their living had suddenly turned enemy, partly that so wide an area and so many communities were so tragically affected and partly that this was a part of the world whose beauty had previously appeared to be so tranquil (and so had welcomed westerners on holiday). The Sunday after the tragedy saw Christian preachers entering their pulpits knowing that they had to try to make some sense of it. A preacher who wanted to do that and yet also felt that it was important still to preach on one of the set readings might have found the Chrysostom method useful.

After perhaps a text (which could be John 1.14 – 'And the Word became flesh and lived among us, and we have seen his glory, the glory as of a father's only son, full of grace and truth'), the first part of the sermon would need to identify with and to address the congregation's feelings about the tsunami. This introduction would lead to a narration, looking back at an event that had dominated the news of the previous week and acknowledging that the event raised questions of theodicy which could not be minimized; even though it would be possible to argue that human carelessness and selfishness had played their parts (there was no early warning system and some of the devastated communities had been built up in unsuitable places to satisfy the desires of western tourists), this awful thing had happened because that is the way that the world is. In some way, 'God who made the earth, the air, the sky, the sea'[37] seemed to be directly or indirectly responsible for the tragedy, and believers had to ask how they could continue to assert that this same God cared for his people. The preacher could close this part of the sermon with the assertion that we ask these questions as believers who are still in the season of Christmas.

The middle section of the sermon would be a commentary on the appointed Gospel passage, John 1.10–18, beginning with a reminder that this picks up the evangelist's reflection on what the incarnation means and stresses the identification of the Creator with his creation. The creative Word 'was in the world and the world came into being through him; yet the world did not know him'. He was rejected by Herod, who tried to kill him, as he would be rejected by the Romans. Worse, 'He came to what was his own, and his own people did not accept him.' Those who claimed that they had been waiting for him failed to recognize him, though not all of them. Some accepted that he was who he claimed to be and put their faith in him, and so became 'children of God, who were born, not of blood or of the will of the flesh or of the will of man, but of God'. Into those few verses, the preacher can point out, the whole of the gospel narrative is effectively compressed.

The preacher then turns to the second half of the lection, in which John asks his readers to contemplate the enormity of the claim: 'The Word became flesh and lived among us, and we have seen his glory, the glory as of a father's only son, full of grace and truth.' The preacher wants to spend some time exploring the verb 'lived' (with its literal meaning of 'made his dwelling'). The sense of tent or tabernacle can be drawn out as can the allusion to the tabernacle where God's glory was revealed in the exodus

---

37 *The School Hymnbook of the Methodist Church*, London: Methodist Youth Department, 45.

narrative. Exodus provides an important point of contrast with the gospel here. With the birth of Jesus, a new way by which humans relate to God the Father Almighty has been inaugurated. Without the incarnation, the relationship was one of law. God's will was disclosed to his people and they tried to live according to it. With the incarnation, law has been replaced by grace, God himself has been disclosed (as the preacher tries to interpret the notoriously difficult final verse), and we have the privilege of living in the light of that revelation.

The transition point to the final part of the sermon is the assertion of the change that the incarnation accomplishes. John's proclamation is of a birth that makes known the true relationship of God and his creation, not as an absentee landlord but as one who takes up residence among us. The preacher returns the focus to verse 14 and to the verb 'tabernacled'. There is an implicit vulnerability in the incarnation. Life is fragile. We cannot hope to make sense of a tragedy like the tsunami, but we can see the creating and caring God as the one in the tent that he pitched in our midst.

2

A WALK THROUGH THE LECTION

The Venerable Bede

Chrysostom exercised his preaching ministry with the presence of the Emperor a constant factor. The Roman Empire had apparently recovered its strength after the disasters of the third century and seemed to be entering into a new golden age inaugurated by Constantine and continued by his sons, a golden age of which the Church was to be a part. But if that were how things seemed in Constantinople, the golden age was to prove short-lived in the western empire (where Constantine had first gathered his armies). By the end of the fourth century, Roman power in the west was collapsing and troops were being withdrawn from the more remote provinces, one of which was the island of Britain. This withdrawal was in the wake of attacks from tribes (whom the Romans called barbarians) who were migrating from the east and settling in various parts of Western Europe, amongst them the Franks, the Vandals, the Lombards and the Saxons. Living outside the Roman Empire, these peoples had remained to a large degree untouched by the imperial religion, Christianity. (The exceptions were the Goths, who had received a form of Christianity from Arian evangelists exiled from the Empire.)

The consequence of this was that the role of the Church in the West changed. The election of an imperial civil servant, Ambrose, as bishop of Milan stands as a signal of the confluence of civic and ecclesiastical administration and interest. The Church was becoming the continuing face of the Empire, as in many places the responsibilities of the collapsing Roman government came to be shouldered by the local bishop. So, for example, Pope Leo I (440–61) found himself negotiating peace treaties with the Huns while sending representatives to the Council of Chalcedon; the burden of coping administratively with the plague which devastated Rome in the late sixth century seems to have fallen on Pope Gregory I (590–604). Catholic Christianity was by now an integral part of society in what had been the western half of the Roman Empire. Unsurprisingly, the tribes that settled in what had been Roman provinces came into contact with the faith and over the course of time adopted it as their religion. By the eighth century, this Christianization had been accomplished to a large degree, not only in the areas where Roman influence was still strongly felt (such as Gaul and Italy) but also in what had been the outposts of the Empire (such as Britain). The Church's achievement was due to a mixture of heroic evangelization and adroit diplomatic manoeuvring, as for a tribe to become Christian there was one person who needed to be converted, the king (which in effect meant that the leading warriors on whom the king depended for his position had also to be persuaded of the wisdom of the course of action). The most detailed example we have of this process comes from England, in the story of the conversion of Edwin, king of the Deirans:

> When he heard this, the king answered it was his will as well as his duty to accept the Faith that Paulinus taught, but said that he must still discuss the matter with his principal advisers and friends, so that, if they were in agreement with him, they might all be cleansed together in Christ, the Fount of Life. Paulinus agreed, and the king kept his promise. He summoned a council of the wise men, and asked each in his turn

his opinion of this strange doctrine and this new way of worshipping the godhead that was being proclaimed to them.

Coifi, the chief priest, replied without hesitation: 'Your Majesty, let us give careful consideration to this new teaching; for I frankly admit that, in my experience, the religion that we have hitherto professed seems valueless and powerless. None of your subjects has been more devoted to the service of our gods than myself; yet there are many to whom you show greater favour, who receive greater honour, and are more successful in their undertakings. Now, if the gods had any power, they would surely have favoured myself, who have been more zealous in their service. Therefore, if on examination you perceive that these new teachings are better and more effectual, let us not hesitate to accept them.

Another of the king's chief men signified his agreement with this prudent argument, and went on to say: 'Your Majesty, when we compare the present life of man on earth with that time of which we have no knowledge, it seems to me like the swift flight of a single sparrow through the banqueting-hall where you are sitting on a winter's day with your thegns and counsellors. In the midst there is a comforting fire to warm the hall; outside the storms of winter rain or snow are raging. The sparrow flies swiftly in through one door of the hall, and out through another. While he is inside he is safe from the winter storms; but after a few moments of comfort, he vanishes from sight into the wintry world from which he came. Even so, man appears on earth for a little while; but of what went before this life or of what follows, we know nothing. Therefore, if this new teaching has brought more certain knowledge, it seems only right that we should follow it.' The other elders and counsellors of the king, under God's guidance, gave similar advice.[1]

One of the notable features of that account is the demand for teaching which is implicit in it. The task of the Church in

---

1 Bede, *Ecclesiastical History* II, 13 (tr. L. Sherley-Price, *Bede: Ecclesiastical History of the English People*, 3rd edn, London: Penguin, 1990, pp. 129f.).

Northumbria over subsequent years would be to extend the conversion by expounding the message briefly expressed in the initial contact with would-be converts. How this was accomplished
is still the subject of research, but it is clear that the main responsibility, at least in England, was borne by a monastic church.
When Gregory I wished to realize his dream of the conversion
of the English, he sent Augustine and a group of monks.[2] When
Oswald wished to re-evangelize Northumbria, he sent to the
monastery of Iona for help.[3] The monasteries were mission bases,
from which monks would be sent out, sometimes alone but usually in pairs or larger groups, to preach for a time in an area.[4]
By these monastic visits, a population that had only the rudi-
ments of the faith would have their knowledge and understanding periodically reinforced and deepened, a process for which we
have epigraphical record in the great stone crosses (such as that
at Ruthwell) which display biblical stories in pictorial form for
the (presumably) unlettered and (possibly) unpastored.

This mission inevitably affected the preaching that was heard
in abbey churches. Whether or not the local population joined
the monks to hear mass and a sermon cannot be determined
with certainty; what is clear, when we look at the homilies of
the Venerable Bede (our prime example of monastic preaching in
this period), is that in the main the preacher's audience was made
up of the other members of his community. Among the monks
who heard the sermons on Sundays and festival days would, we
can safely presume, be those who would be sent out during the
week to share their faith with the unlettered in the villages. The
task of the preacher in the abbey church was, therefore, to teach
the teachers, to equip these evangelists with a thorough understanding of the Scriptures which could form the basis of their
own ministry.

Bede (who lived from 673 to 735) was one who undertook that
task. Through his *Ecclesiastical History of the English People,*

---

2 Bede, *Ecclesiastical History* I, 23 (*op. cit.*, p. 72).

3 Bede, *Ecclesiastical History* III, 3 (*op. cit.*, p. 146).

4 Bede, *The Life of Cuthbert*, ch. 8 (ed. & tr. B. Colgrave, *Two Lives of Cuthbert*, Cambridge: Cambridge University Press, 1940, p. 187).

he is our main source for the history of England in the sixth and seventh centuries. Bede's main theme was the development of the English as a recognizably Christian people; military and political events are only of interest to him inasmuch as they favoured or hindered the spread of the gospel. Consequently, through Bede we see the process of evangelization by which, region by region, the Church brought into its fold the different regional tribes (the Deirans, the East Anglians, the South Saxons and others), and we are introduced to the missionary heroes of that process (Aidan, Cuthbert, Chad, Cedd and Wilfrid). Bede was a meticulous historian; the quality of his work was the reason for its immense popularity throughout the Middle Ages, and the diligence of his method means that he (unlike some other mediaeval writers) is still highly regarded by historians today. 'The skill with which Bede organized his material and arranged his narrative, together with the critical acumen that he displays, makes him by far the greatest of writers of history in the early medieval West.'[5]

Bede, however, did not regard himself primarily as a historian. To the last chapter of the *Ecclesiastical History* he appended an autobiographical note from which we learn that he had been entrusted to the monks of Monkwearmouth-Jarrow at the age of seven. 'I have spent all the remainder of my life in this monastery,' he wrote, 'and devoted myself entirely to the study of the Scriptures.'[6] He published the fruits of his study for the benefit of others and his output was prodigious. The vast majority of the works are biblical, mainly commentaries of one form or another; he also penned a number of saints' lives, a book of hymns, studies of the art of writing and works of science. Bede was a man of enquiring mind. For him, for example, it was not enough in his martyrology to record the dates on which a martyr was to be commemorated but 'also by what king of combat and under what judge' they died.[7]

Among his works that Bede lists are 'two books of homilies on

---

5 R. Collins, 'Bede' in K. Boyd (ed.), *Encyclopedia of Historians and Historical Writing*, vol 1., London and Chicago: Fitzroy Dearborn, 1999, p. 87.

6 Bede, *Ecclesiastical History*, V, 24 (*op. cit.*, p. 329).

7 Bede, *Ecclesiastical History*, V, 24 (*op. cit.*, p. 329).

the gospels'. It seems likely that these were the texts of sermons delivered in the abbey church at Jarrow at mass on Sundays or major feasts.[8] P. J. West has shown how the language and style of the Easter homilies were constructed by Bede to fit with the liturgical setting of the vigil and other ceremonies.[9] That they were listed as published works suggests that they were circulated within Bede's own lifetime, and they may have been altered for publication. It might be that Bede himself was not always the preacher of his own homilies;[10] it has been noted that Bede does not provide a homily for a text on which Gregory the Great had furnished one,[11] which might lead us to conclude that it was common practice for Gregory's homilies to be read at many of the monastery services and that Bede's were intended to complete the collection. Gregory was held in high esteem in the early Anglo-Saxon Church, celebrated as the apostle of the nation,[12] and was the conduit through which much patristic scholarship was mediated to the English monks. Gregory (unsurprisingly) was the greatest influence on Bede and on Bede's homiletic ministry. Like his mentor, Bede saw preaching as expounding the Scriptures.

Bede's sermons followed the patristic pattern of working through a portion of Scripture. According to Benedicta Ward, 'it is hardly possible to distinguish [in Bede] between homily and commentary'.[13] Martin and Hurst, however, notice a crucial difference, and one which marks Bede out from Gregory also. Bede's commentaries are filled with quotations from the Fathers; Bede did not see himself (and did not want to see himself) as an innovator. He was firmly in line with the catholic orthodoxy that he had been taught, and so his task in writing a commentary was to note the acquired wisdom about each verse. There are no such

8 L. T. Martin and D. Hurst OSB (*Bede the Venerable: Homilies on the Gospels*, vol. 1, Kalamazoo: Cistercian Publications, 1991, pp. xif.) disagree.

9 P. J. West, 'Liturgical Style and Structure in Bede's Homily for the Easter Vigil', *American Benedictine Review* 23 (1972), pp. 1–8.

10 Martin and Hurst, *op. cit.*, vol. 1, p. xi.

11 Martin and Hurst, *op. cit.*, vol. 1, p. xvi.

12 B. Colgrave, *The Earliest Life of Gregory the Great*, Cambridge: Cambridge University Press, 1968, p. 19.

13 Benedicta Ward SLG, *The Venerable Bede*, London: Geoffrey Chapman, 1990, p. 64.

quotations in the homilies, although Bede remains heavily dependent on those who had gone before him,[14] especially Augustine
and Gregory. In Bede's homilies, almost the only references other
than from the text under consideration are to other books in the
Bible.

That gives us a clue to his method, which is a pedagogical one
familiar to anyone who was at school in England in the 1960s
and 70s (and very possibly at other periods). It is a method that
may, however, not have been experienced by those who received
their primary education more recently. It is an oft-heard lament
from those involved in education in Britain that the demands of
the national curriculum (and its cousin, a regime of compulsory
testing) have left teachers with less freedom. One of the examples of this which is often trotted out at this point in the lament
is the class ramble. On a pleasant afternoon a teacher would say
to (usually) her class, 'Let's go for a walk.' Coats were donned,
pupils were instructed to arm themselves with pencils and paper,
and the teacher led the way around the school grounds or along
the roads to a field, a park or possibly a river bank. All the
way along the journey, the teacher would point out to the class
features of the area which were of interest. Many, possibly most,
concerned natural phenomena. Children would learn the names
of trees and how to recognize them by their leaves, fruit or bark,
there would be attempts to identify the song of a bird, the signs
of the changing seasons would be observed and duly noted, a
remarkable cloud formation would be admired. Sometimes this
study would drift into folklore, with the various fantastical
explanations for the prevalence of mushrooms in an patch of
grass being related, or ancient rhymes being recited as the seeds
of a clock dandelion were blown to the wind (to the delight later,
no doubt, of the custodians of nearby gardens). Not all the detail
was about natural history, however. The vapour trail of an aero-
plane, the meaning of a road sign, or the mechanics of a crane
on a nearby building site might be the subject of discussion.
Nor was it all simply informative; there was often an imperative
side to the afternoon as well, with caution being given about

---

14 Martin and Hurst, *op. cit.*, p. xiii.

the dangers of eating leaves, berries or fungi, or playing near deep water or railway lines, and with practical and memorable instruction on crossing the road safely being rehearsed.

Bede the preacher is Bede the teacher, and he walks us through a passage of Scripture in each of his sermons much as a primary school teacher would walk her class through a local area. Like the teacher, Bede does not only have one sort of material that he wants to observe in the homily. Bede inherited a tradition which saw the Bible as having a range of meanings which it was the task of the exegete to disclose. Hermeneutics for Bede operated in four ways and, in a letter which introduced his commentary on the books of Samuel, Bede expounded what he believed those four ways to be: 'The word of the heavenly oracle can be received in either an historical, or allegorical, a tropological (that is, moral) or even an anagogical sense.'[15] Bede goes on to explain what he means by each of those terms.

The historical sense is the most straightforward and, as we have seen, was the sense favoured by the Antiochene school of which Chrysostom was a representative. A text would have lying behind it some historical facts of interest which needed to be understood literally. Bede the exegete was always also Bede the historian, and his homilies could develop detailed historical explanations of a text. For example, in his sermon on the birth of John the Baptist,[16] Bede pauses at the information that Zechariah was a priest in the division of Abijah to explain who Abijah was. This entails a brief summary of the history of the priesthood before the time of David, the Davidic reforms (as recorded in 1 Chronicles 23–24), and the drawing of lots among the divisions of the priesthood to determine the order in which they served. Bede had made himself something of an expert on the detail of Old Testament worship and (as often) is led from a historical excursus to another (allegorical) point. Another example of his historical reading comes in the same sermon when Bede notes that the barrenness of Elizabeth parallels that of Sarah, the wife of Manoah and Hannah. It is important, Bede is arguing, that

---

15 Quoted in Ward, *op. cit.*, p. 49.
16 Bede, *Homilies*, II, 19 (*op. cit.*, pp. 188–201).

these examples are read literally, because only by doing so can it be clear that grace is in operation in the birth of their children.

Allegorical interpretation of the Scriptures (generally speaking the contribution of the Alexandrian Fathers in distinction from the Antiochene methods typical of Chysostom) was a key element in the mediaeval Church's understanding of the unity of the Old and New Testaments because it found value in Old Testament texts which were to be understood as prefiguring Christ or his Church. Bede's expertise in Old Testament worship had led to the production of two works – one on the tabernacle of Moses and one on the temple of Solomon – which were replete with allegorical detail. In his sermon on the dedication of a church, he draws on this scholarship and asks why there needed to be two places of the Old Covenant when Christ only has one Church. 'No-one should think it incongruous . . . Two dwellings were fashioned to signify the two peoples who would come together in the same faith, the Jews and the gentiles.'[17] To modern ears (assuming that the tent's preceding the temple is simply an indication of the historic development of the Hebrews from nomadic tribes to settled people under a monarchy), this sort of interpretation might sound contrived and unnecessary, but for Bede and for many of his predecessors it was a staple of exegesis. The allegorical approach saw every detail, and particularly every number, mentioned in the Scriptures as having some meaning beyond, or beneath, that which was obvious.[18]

Bede notes that there are two sorts of tropological or moral interpretation to be found in Scripture, related to the previous two methods. A verse can be a literal injunction, a text that enjoins one sort of behaviour or prohibits another; so, for example, Bede begins his homily on the feast of Peter and Paul (for which the text was Jesus' conversation with Peter in John 21), 'The present reading from the holy gospel commends to us the virtue of perfect love.'[19] In other cases, the imperative is reached by an allegorical method. So, in interpreting the story of the wise

---

17. Bede, *Homilies*, II, 25 (*op. cit.*, p. 256).
18 Bede, *Homilies*, I, 14 (*op. cit.*, pp. 134–47).
19 Bede, *Homilies*, II, 22 (*op. cit.*, p. 220).

man building his house on the rock, Bede tells us that the man is Jesus who built his house (Church) on a rock (Peter). Therefore, the instruction to the disciple (or latter-day believer) was to imitate Christ in all that he or she does. Only that way can a person withstand the storms that batter the house (which Bede interprets as temptations).[20]

Finally, Bede finds an anagogical meaning in some parts of Scripture. Anagogy, Bede explains, is that which refers to the future blessings which await the elect and the punishments which are prepared for those who reject the message of the gospel. Again, for Bede, texts interpreted anagogically can have both a literal and an allegorical sense. So, for example, in a sermon on part of the Last Supper discourses,[21] Bede reflects on Jesus' words to the disciples that they will be sorrowful while the world rejoices but that their sorrow would turn to joy. That, Bede tells his congregation, was not only true of the disciples over the subsequent three days but is the perennial condition of the Church which sorrows when evil triumphs in this world but will see fortunes reversed in the next.

Bede was neither the first nor the last to read Scripture in this fourfold way. It remained a method in common use until at least the sixteenth century, as the rhyme from that period shows:

> The letter shows us what God and our fathers did;
> The allegory shows us where our faith is hid;
> The moral gives rules for daily life;
> The anagogy shows us where we end our strife.[22]

In his homilies, Bede uses all of these methods, often all four in one sermon, moving seamlessly from one to another. A good example of this is his homily on the cleansing of the temple (John 2.12–22).[23] There is no introduction to a Bede homily; he simply steps into the text and begins his guided tour. In this instance there are about a dozen stops along the way, when teacher draws

---

20 Bede, *Homilies*, II, 25 (*op. cit.*, pp. 255–68).

21 Bede, *Homilies*, II, 13 (*op. cit.*, pp. 117–23).

22 Quoted in R. M. Grant and D. Tracey, *A Short History of the Interpretation of the Bible*, London: SCM Press, 1984, p. 85.

23 Bede, Homilies, II, 1 (*op. cit.*, pp. 1–12).

the pupils' attention to something, literally, allegorically, tropo-
logically or anagogically.

The first point that Bede feels he needs to make is a historical
one. Jesus is recorded as going down to Capernaum with his
mother, his brothers, and his disciples. Bede immediately sets out
to quash any notion that the perpetual virginity of Mary, the
mother of the Lord, is in doubt. It is even heresy in Bede's eyes to
suppose that these brothers are the children of Joseph by another
(presumably earlier) wife. The explanation of this curiosity is
that the term brothers could be used to denote those of a kindred
relationship beyond the immediate family, and Bede rehearses
a number of instances when the word is employed in the Old
Testament with reference to cousins or nephews.

Bede's next word is one of moral injunction. Jesus went to
Jerusalem for the Passover. That he was careful to observe the
requirements of his religion should be an example to his followers not to neglect their own attention to the worship of the
Church. Whether Bede had in mind some of his contemporaries,
perhaps even some of his own congregation, who were less than
diligent in their attendance at mass, we have no way of knowing,
though in his letter to Egbert, Bede did have cause to lament the
lax forms of monastic life which were proliferating in England in
the early eighth century.[24]

Bede moves on; even the language that he uses suggests the
teacher leading an observation ('let us see what he found . . .').
The scene in the temple is explored from a number of angles –
there is the historical explanation of why the beasts and birds are
there, there is a moral injunction to respect a house of prayer and
there is an anagogical interpretation of the whip that Jesus made,
which comes to represent the punishment that the unrepentant
can expect after judgement. These themes are woven together in
this section of the sermon. Bede then tackles a historical detail,
the fact that John tells this story at the beginning of Jesus' ministry whilst the Synoptics place it in Holy Week. He understands
this to mean that Jesus cleansed the temple twice; the temple
now moves in Bede's thinking to become the Church and then

---

24 Bede, *Letter to Egbert*, 11 (tr. D. Farmer in Sherley-Price, *op. cit.*, p. 346).

(by allusion to baptism) every individual Christian, and the story becomes a terrible warning that a visitation might occur at any time. Particularly to be afraid are those who are found (in an allegorical aside) ministering in the church for worldly gain.

This has become the main theme of the homily. If the hearers take away nothing else, they will be left with the message that we are the temple of God and the church in which we worship is a temple and we need to behave accordingly. But at this point, something else catches teacher's eye, and Bede has a theological point to make. The words of Jesus describing the temple as his father's house stress (to Bede's ear) the divine Sonship. The first verse of the lection, mentioning his mother, stresses Jesus' humanity. For Bede, we cannot 'pass over' (a favourite Bede term) the fact that the Bible is reminding us of the two natures of Jesus. One of Bede's central concerns was to maintain the orthodoxy of the young Anglo-Saxon Church and so an opportunity to nail his colours firmly to a Chalcedonian mast could not be missed. With that digression over, Bede returns to the text and to his main theme, with a moral exhortation. As Jesus was consumed with zeal for his Father's house, so Christians should be zealous about the purity of the temple.

The remainder of the sermon (about half of it) revolves around a controlling typology. As John identifies the temple with the body of Jesus (John 2.21), so Bede identifies the body of Jesus with the Church. It is hard not to wonder if Bede's hearers were as fascinated as he clearly was with the detail of the building of the temple; it may well be that there were mutterings in the cloister on the subject of their preacher's apparent obsession. In this part of the sermon Bede uses the full range of his allegorical method when he comes to the number 46 (the number of years that Jesus' interlocutors claim it had taken to build the temple he was threatening to destroy). Literally, Bede takes this to refer to the delays in the building programme of Nehemiah (and not, as modern commentators do, to the rebuilding project undertaken in the time of Herod the Great).[25] But allegorically,

---

25 G. O'Day, 'The Gospel of John', *New Interpreter's Bible*, vol. 9, Nashville: Abingdon Press, 1995, p. 544.

following Augustine's theory on the development of the foetus,[26] 46 becomes a symbol of perfection – the 46th day after conception (according to the ancients) was the day on which formation was complete and growth began. This confirms Bede in his freedom to move along the axis he has created for himself (Temple – Body of Jesus – Church) and he now takes his congregation into the Jerusalem temple to point out features of interest. All four types of interpretation jostle with each other and, in the most elaborate paragraphs, come back on themselves to form a circuit. So, when Bede notes that there was a door in the side of the temple, he reminds his congregation of the piercing of the side of the crucified Christ which in turn symbolizes the water of baptism and the wine of the Eucharist which are themselves the means by which the faithful ascend to the life of heaven, like the pilgrims who climbed up to the door in the side of the temple.

The conclusion to the homily takes us, as it were, back into the classroom of discipleship. Jesus' actions in the temple prefigured his death and resurrection. The congregation are in Lent preparing for the Triduum, so they are exhorted to cleanse themselves that they may become dwelling places for the Holy Spirit. The sermon ends (as do most of Bede's sermons) with a Trinitarian doxology.

Throughout the Middle Ages, preachers continued to use this form of homily. Working through the Scriptures verse by verse, it became known as the postil (from the Latin *post illa*, 'after that'). Bede was recognized as a master of the form. His homilies move through the text pausing at length on some verses and passing swiftly by others with a recognition of the needs of his congregation. His strength came not just from the mastery of the form but from his intimate acquaintance with the fourfold method and his wide reading of the Fathers. One of the many epithets which later Anglo-Saxons bestowed on Bede is *candela ecclesiae*, and it is not difficult from a reading of his homilies to see its appropriateness. Bede's aim was to illuminate the Church; his carefully crafted homilies shone light on and from the Scriptures in the Anglo-Saxon Church that was still finding its way.

---

26 Martin and Hurst, *op. cit.*, vol. 2, p. 8.

Of all the forms of preaching explored in this book, Bede's may, at first sight, seem the one least suitable to be adopted by a preacher in the twenty-first century. The fourfold method of interpretation on which the whole homiletical approach depends has long since fallen out of favour. Congregations would look askance at being told that the man healed at the Pool of Beth-saida (John 5.1–18) represented the wicked sinner because the 38 years of his infirmity indicates (by being 2 short of 40) lack of love for both God and neighbour.[27] But the problem there lies with Bede's content and not with the form in which that content is presented. It could be argued that the form is entirely appropriate for a modern sermon, although there are contemporary homileticians who would resist the pedagogical approach implicit in Bede's homilies, arguing that preaching and teaching are distinct activities in Christian ministry.[28] However, with caveats, the method that Bede adopted in the eighth century might still find its place in the twenty-first. As is discussed in Chapter 8, modern homileticians encourage an approach that works with, rather than across, the narrative flow of the text. Stephen Wright calls it 'preaching with the grain of Scripture'.[29] 'Going with the grain', he argues, enables the preacher 'to be a companion to listeners on a journey *through* Scripture – like Jesus with the disciples on the Emmaus Road.'

There are other reasons why such an approach might work well in the early twenty-first century. It is often noted by scholars that Bede's sermons resemble his commentaries in their approach to the text; in the same way, the sort of approach that is outlined here, working through a passage of Scripture verse by verse, may seem more appropriate to a Bible study, where the leader guides a group through a text which they have before them. It may be that preachers who want to develop their congregation's famil-iarity with and understanding of Scripture could do that from

---

27 Bede, *Homilies*, op. cit., pp. 224f.

28 But see against this view John H. Westerhoff, 'Teaching and Preaching', in W. H. Willimon and R. Lischer (eds), *Concise Encyclopedia of Preaching*, Louis-ville: Westminster John Knox Press, 1995, pp. 467ff.

29 *Preaching with the Grain of Scripture*, Cambridge: Grove Books, 2001, p. 11.

the pulpit. In many churches Bible study groups are attended only by a very small minority of the membership and any expectation that members should be part of such activities is often unrealized. The Sunday service may be the only opportunity that the preacher or minister has to invite the congregation to engage with the Bible. Bede's method of repeating every verse of the lection in the homily might not find favour with modern preachers or listeners, but there is no reason why the congregation should not have the text before them. In many places they already do, either in pew Bibles or printouts of the lectionary. We live in a highly literate society; more people can read in western countries than at any other period in history, so preaching might reasonably be seen once again as an invitation to the congregation to walk through the text with the preacher.

That more people can read than ever before does not, however, mean that more people do read than ever before. Part of the reason for that is that we live in an age of audiovisual technology and receive information not only from the printed page but from radio and television and increasingly from computer screens. Churches are coming to terms with this in many places, with data projection of hymn and liturgical texts being increasingly common. That in itself suggests that the time may be ripe to adopt Bede's approach. A preacher could take a text and while 'walking the congregation through it' display the verse under discussion on a screen. The opportunity for supporting each part of the sermon with images is immense, provided those images serve to focus attention on the aspect of the verse being highlighted and not to distract from it. Again, the method has about it echoes of the age of Bede, since his church sought to communicate visually as well as orally. The eighth century saw not only the erection of the great stone crosses (such as that at Ruthwell) but also the celebrated illuminated manuscript of the Lindisfarne Gospels. Images were used to support and to impress on the memory the meaning of words.

The fourfold method of interpreting Scripture has gone (although, as Grant and Tracey have noted, it survived until the sixteenth century),[30] so we would not expect the lengthy

---

30 *op. cit.*, p. 85.

allegorizing of Bede. In a way, though, a modern preacher would want to do something not dissimilar. Parts of the sermon would need to focus on the literal meaning of the words – what happened or what the writer was saying. In the example below, that is the sermon's starting point, as the preacher shares the psalmist's view of creation. Parts of the sermon 'show us where our faith is hid' – in this case, in the cosmological argument. The idea of a moral element to preaching might not commend itself to some ears, but parts of the sermon have to be application – the preacher is answering the implied question 'What must we do?' Fourth, the preacher would still want to note the hints of heaven that a passage offers. With all those four purposes in mind, the preacher then moves through the text as if on a walk, using the Scripture as a series of windows – sometimes into wider biblical themes (in this case, creation and grace), sometimes into contemporary issues (in this case the environment), sometimes into controversy (in this case with militant atheism), sometimes into theological or spiritual matters (the call to holiness and the need for humility).

Bede's homilies are on the Gospels, but there are other parts of Scripture which might lend themselves as comfortably to this approach. In this example, the preacher takes one of the psalms and walks through it with the congregation. The psalm is 19; the sermon might begin with the preacher inviting the congregation to look at the screen on which would be displayed a series of pictures of the night sky. After a moment of silence, the first verse is displayed:

The heavens declare the glory of God,
and the firmament shows his handiwork.

Throughout the sermon, the verses of the psalm appear on the screen at appropriate points (suitably set against powerful imagery – in the first six verses, scenes of the sky).

The preacher begins with a reflection on the power of creation to communicate to us something of the existence of the Creator, pointing out that this is no new idea –

One day tells its tale to another and one night imparts knowledge to another

– but that versions of the cosmological argument date from antique times. Paul, attempting to stop people venerating Barnabas and himself as gods, spoke of the one Creator who 'has not left himself without a witness'.[31] Not everyone has picked up on this clue; the silent eloquence that is the God-witnessing majesty of creation –

Although they have no words or language,
and their voices are not heard,
Their sound has gone out into all lands,
and their message to the ends of the world

– has not been heard by all. Perhaps Richard Dawkins is right – the argument can never prove that God exists to those determined to be deaf. But to those who believe, there is a message as to the nature of God.

It is a message that can be heard in every aspect of creation. The psalmist takes one example –

In the deep has he set a pavilion for the sun;
it comes forth like a bridegroom out of his chamber;
it rejoices like a champion to run its course.
It goes forth from the uttermost edge of the heavens
and runs about to the end of it again;
nothing is hidden from its burning heat.

– which the preacher explores, mixing modern scientific knowledge about the sun, its power and the dependence of the whole solar system on it, with the imagery employed by the psalmist – the bragging husband or the successful sportsman. Small wonder the ancients worshipped the sun; its power astounds us, yet it is only a small part of the creation of an infinitely greater God.

As, continues the preacher, is the human being. So the preacher turns with the psalmist to ask where we fit in to the creation that

31 Acts 14.17.

sings God's praise. The preacher explores the psalmist's instinctive response – to turn to Torah.

> The law of the LORD is perfect and revives the soul;
> the testimony of the LORD is sure
> and gives wisdom to the innocent.
> The statutes of the LORD are just and rejoice the heart;
> the commandment of the LORD is clear
> and gives light to the eyes.
> The fear of the LORD is clean and endures for ever;
> the judgments of the LORD are true and righteous altogether.

The imagery on the screen changes to scenes of social unrest and environmental damage as the preacher asks the congregation to look around at God's world and see what has happened to it. The yearning which the psalmist expresses for the Law is a yearning to live in harmony with creation (and therefore with the will of the Creator), not in opposition to it. As the projected images change to those things which are far more pleasant –

> More to be desired are they than gold,
> more than much fine gold,
> sweeter far than honey,
> than honey in the comb

– the preacher reflects on the way in which the environmental movement has struck a chord with those outside the Church. The philosopher's stone of the twenty-first century is a green lifestyle.

What the psalmist recognized is that living in tune with God's creation is good for the creature.

> By them also is your servant enlightened,
> and in keeping them there is great reward.

The preacher might refer to recent studies that suggest that religious practice is good for one's health, but the congregation cannot be complacent. Our frailty and our apparently inexhaustible capacity to sin have to be acknowledged.

> Who can tell how often he offends?

The good news which this sermon proclaims is that grace is available from God who knows us better than we know ourselves.

> Cleanse me from my secret faults.
> Above all, keep your servant from presumptuous sins;
> let them not get dominion over me;
> then shall I be whole and sound,
> and innocent of a great offence.

The sermon ends with a final reflection on the balance of all creation, the marvel by which the earth's distance from the sun enables it to sustain life. The believer is called to be in tune with that balance; in humility we receive the grace that enables that to happen.

> Let the words of my mouth and the meditation of my heart be acceptable in your sight,
> O Lord, my strength and my redeemer.

3

THE SECOND PART OF RHETORIC

'Natural Architecture' in the Middle Ages

> The first of rhetoric's parts is the wise choice of matter,
> And clearly the second is the proper arrangement of thoughts;
> The third, a difficult task, demands the use of appropriate language;
> Memory's fourth – be master of what you would say.
> Then, fifth, be eloquent; this makes the system perfect.[1]

So Walafrid Strabo eulogized in the early ninth century. The Carolingian renaissance celebrated the classical skills of rhetoric, although Walafrid may have witnessed very little original rhetoric from the pulpit. Whether or not Bede preached his own homilies in the church at Jarrow in the form that we have them,[2] it is certain that they were preached by many others in other places. During the Middle Ages, it became increasingly common for those responsible for the ministry of the word to read a homily of one of the Fathers of the Church rather than dare to offer to their congregations anything that they had prepared themselves. Throughout the early Middle Ages, homiliaries were

---

1 Walafrid Strabo, 'The Five Parts of Rhetoric', tr. J. M. Miller, in Miller et al. (eds), *Readings in Medieval Rhetoric*, Bloomington and London: Indiana University Press, 1973, p. 128.

2 L. T. Martin and D. Hurst OSB, *Bede the Venerable: Homilies on the Gospels*, vol. 1, Kalamazoo, Cistercian Publications, 1991, p. xii.

in circulation, offering for those who needed them ready-made material. The parish clergy clearly felt that it was far above them to study the Scriptures and to produce their own interpretive work. Alfred the Great's expectation that they should know the Creed and the Lord's Prayer seems to the present generation (where it is proposed that all parish clergy should be educated to the equivalent of first degree level)[3] laughably minimalistic. Preaching, however, had never been the particular ministry of parish priests; it was the obligation and privilege of the prelates, the bishops and abbots. By the end of the first millennium, it seems clear that even they were not exercising the responsibility. Anselm of Canterbury's approach in preaching his own sermons in the late twelfth century was regarded as something of a novelty by his contemporaries,[4] and when Guibert of Nogent wrote his 'Book on how a sermon ought to be given'[5] as the preface to his commentary on Genesis, he began by lamenting the reluctance of some of those who ought to preach to do so.

Guibert appears to have broken new ground in this work. Very little had been written about the practice of preaching since Augustine's exhortation to use the art of rhetoric in *De Doctrina Christiana*. Hrabanus Maurus (like Walafrid Strabo a product of the Carolingian renaissance) had penned a work on the duty of the clergy but this contained nothing that was not in Augustine.[6] Guibert, in contrast, was not simply attempting to reproduce the wisdom of the past; his concern was the benefit of the listeners in his own day. He warned preachers not to make their sermons too long or to try to include too many ideas in them and cautioned against the tendency to overdo the use of allegorical interpretation (he found that applying common sense to hermeneutics was of value for both preacher and hearers) and suggested that preachers needed to be aware that listeners came to a sermon

---

3 *Shaping the Future* (Church of England Division of Ministry Report, 2006), p. 80.

4 G. R. Evans, *Alan of Lille: The Frontiers of Theology in the Late Twelfth Century*, Cambridge: Cambridge University Press, 1983, p. 87.

5 Miller et al. (eds), *op. cit.*, pp. 162–81.

6 O. C. Edwards, *A History of Preaching*, vol. 1, Nashville: Abingdon Press, 2004, p. 164.

with different levels of understanding and that all had to be fed. Sermons should analyse the causes of sin in order to offer a remedy to the sinners who were listening and should speak persuasively of the truth of the message. To this end, scholarship was important but so also was the sincerity and personal experience of the preacher; the preacher was not a reporter who could talk about battles without ever having been to war, but one who spoke with 'the real authority of his own spiritual struggles'.[7]

What Guibert did not do was to instruct his readers how to organize their commonsense interpretations and personal testimony into a sermon. It might be presumed that the preaching he envisaged, and to which he was subjected, followed in some way or another the model of the patristic homily. Very few sermons from before Guibert's time have survived in order for us to have any idea. What is clear is that Guibert does not expect (as it would appear Bede did) that the lectionary should drive the sermon. Preachers were to address not the Scripture but the congregation. If Guibert was reflecting a changing understanding, that change becomes clear when we turn to the work of Alan of Lille.

Alan of Lille (*c.* 1128–1202) seems to have pioneered a new genre in theological writing, the *ars praedicandi* (the Art of Preaching). Little is known about Alan's life, other than that he studied and taught at the burgeoning proto-university of Paris, probably from the 1140s onwards. He was a speculative theologian at a time when France was the centre of rapid theological development, and if Paris was to be the academic centre for theology (a position it attained without rival in the thirteenth century) it did so alongside a continuing tradition of monastic theology in which the Cistercians (led by Bernard of Clairvaux) were dominant. That dominance is reflected in Alan's own life; he was involved in the missions against the Cathars in southern France alongside the Cistercians and some time before his death he entered the monastery of Cîteaux. In addition to his work on preaching, Alan made contributions to systematic and pastoral theology, with his *Regulae Theologicae* (in which he argued that Christian doctrine was self-evidently true) and his manual for

---

7 Miller et al. (eds), *op. cit.*, p. 175.

confessors.[8] His most famous work in his own lifetime was his remarkable *Anticlaudianus,* an allegorical work on the redemption of humankind. It appears to have been obscure to some even in his own day,[9] but was remarkably popular, even to the extent of being set to music.[10] Strangely, the author of this bestseller remained without preferment. Whether he himself was ever a preacher is unclear. Gillian Evans believes that he was, though H. O. Old argues that when he joined the Cistercians he did so as a lay brother,[11] so although Alan was clearly quite capable of writing sermons it may have been others who delivered them.

The Art of Preaching clearly shows the way in which theological thinking was developing. It stands, as Alan does, on the threshold of scholasticism. Alan appears to have been the first person to produce a definition of preaching.[12] 'Preaching is an open and public instruction in faith and behaviour, whose purpose is the forming of men; it derives from the path of reason and from the fountainhead of the "authorities".'[13] Alan was aware that he was treading virgin territory here, but he was nothing if not an innovator,[14] whose practice was often to break new ground through allegory. His treatise begins with the analogy of Jacob's ladder, whose first rung is the confession of sin, and which can be ascended through prayer, thanksgiving, Bible study, enquiry about uncertain points in the Scripture from a teacher, and biblical exposition, to the final rung of preaching. Before him, Alan believed, 'various writers have composed treatises on the other "rungs" . . . little has been said up to now

---

8 G. R. Evans, 'Alan of Lille', in W. H. Willimon and R. Lischer (eds), *Concise Encyclopedia of Preaching*, Louisville, KY: Westminster John Knox Press, 1995, p. 9.

9 Evans, *Alan of Lille*, p. viii.

10 Evans, *op. cit.*, p. 1.

11 Evans, *op. cit.*, p. 87; H. O. Old, *The Reading and Preaching of the Scriptures*, Grand Rapids: Wm Eerdmans, vol. 3, 1999, p. 332.

12 R. Lischer (ed.), *The Company of Preachers*, Grand Rapids and Cambridge, UK: Wm Eerdmans, 2002, p. 3.

13 Alan of Lille (tr. G. R. Evans), *The Art of Preaching*, Kalamazoo: Cistercian Publications, 1983, ch. 1.

14 Evans, *Alan of Lille*, p. ix.

about preaching'.[15] What Alan has to say is that preaching is applied theology; his preachers are the angels who ascend the ladder to explore spiritual truths and descend the ladder to offer the ethical guidance that follows from those truths. It therefore needs to be taken seriously, to be free from jest, to be rhetorically pleasing but not overly embroidered with oratorical ornaments. The end of preaching is to make the hearers better Christians, so the preacher must always be aware of the needs of the audience, be wary of shallow emotionalism, and be brief. A sermon must be long enough to make its point but no longer.

Alan's preface is followed by what he suggests are examples, but really are instructions on how to preach. Each follows a similar pattern. Alan begins with the purpose of the sermon (or in the last few the intended audience of the sermon); then comes a text (or more often a number of suggested texts), which is offered as the 'authority' for the sermon. These are overwhelmingly scriptural references, although patristic authorities are sometimes included amongst the alternatives, and in one instance there is even a suggestion from Seneca.[16] As becomes clear, these are not texts (as a later preacher might understand them) to be expounded in the sermon; rather, their function is to indicate that the topic of the sermon is one which was taken seriously by the biblical writers and is being treated in harmony with Scripture. Alan then recommends a way of addressing the subject, usually, but by no means invariably, by dividing it into a number of sub-sections. So, he suggests that sermons be preached on the three kinds of envy,[17] the three kinds of vanity,[18] the three kinds of anger,[19] and the seven kinds of patience.[20] The aim of the sermon is then (and Alan offers hints at examples to support the argument) to encourage the congregation to shun the sin or embrace the virtue. In some of his sketches, the division of the subject will be paralleled by the division of the application; so,

---

15 Alan, *op. cit.*, preface.
16 *op. cit.*, ch. 24.
17 *op. cit.*, ch. 8.
18 *op. cit.*, ch. 2.
19 *op. cit.*, ch. 9.
20 *op. cit.*, ch. 15.

for example, there are three kinds of fortitude and there are three kinds of misfortune which fortitude can overcome.[21]

With his contribution to the practical needs of the preacher and his involvement in preaching against the Albigensian heresy in the south of France, Gillian Evans suggests that Alan was a man ahead of his time and would in the next century have been one of the Friars Preachers.[22] At the time of his death, the Cistercian mission with which he had been associated was making little progress. In 1206, an Augustinian canon, Domingo de Guzman, was sent to be a part of that effort, and recognized that a different sort of preacher was needed if Catholicism was to win its case. His thinking led to the creation of a new form of Augustinian order, recognized in 1221 as the Order of Preachers, but soon known more commonly as the Dominicans. In parallel to the Spanish Dominic (Domingo) sending out mendicants to preach the gospel, an Italian, Giovanni Bernadone (known to his friends as Francesco), was experimenting with evangelical poverty in a similar way. His was a new order, the Friars Minor, though again quickly known by the name of their founder, Franciscans. Preaching and thinking about preaching in the thirteenth century were to be dominated by the members of these two new, rapidly growing orders.

The rise of the mendicant orders cannot be understood in isolation from two major changes which were under way in mediaeval society at the time. One was the growth of the towns. After the turn of the millennium, Europe entered a period of comparative peace as the series of raids and invasions that had characterized European history came to an end. With peace came economic prosperity; the resulting surplus meant that fewer people were needed in the production of sufficient food, so that more could live away from farming. Trade flourished in the new environment and with trade came an increase in manufacturing. So, all over Europe, and especially in Italy and the Low Countries, there was a migration into walled settlements. Existing conurbations

---

21 *op. cit.*, ch. 24.
22 Evans, *Alan of Lille*, p. 12.

grew in size, and smaller communities came to have their own independent identity and to acquire charters. Feudal society was giving way to something more complex, in which merchants began to take their place alongside landowners in the ranks of the wealthy.[23] Francis, of course, was a scion of this new mercantile elite, and the mendicant orders grew up in urban soil.[24] Much of the preaching of the friars was to the growing ranks of the town-dwellers, some of them impoverished by the rapid social change of the period, some of them wealthy and looking for social advancement. Whether or not there was any expectation that the parish clergy had a duty to preach to these people is not clear; what happened was that the friars embraced the opportunity to share in what had traditionally been the bishops' ministry. Dominicans and (after Francis) Franciscans recognized that if they were to exercise the ministry effectively, they needed to be trained and prepared for it.

That identified need was one of the causes of the second great change in the thirteenth century – the growth of the universities. It was no accident that the leading names among the 'schoolmen' of the generations after Alan were mendicants, among them Albert the Great, Thomas Aquinas and Bonaventure. Neither is it an accident that the proliferation of writing about preaching in the thirteenth and fourteenth centuries, and the great number of *artes praedicandi*,[25] came from the pens of the friars. Not only were there books on how to preach, there were also in circulation collections of *exempla* to illustrate sermons, and the Franciscans may have carried pocket books of model sermons to help them to prepare as they travelled.[26] The surviving manuscript evidence suggests that the mendicant preacher of the later Middle Ages had no shortage of resources. Friars were determined to encourage each other to preach and to preach well.

---

23 M. Barber, *The Two Cities*, London & New York: Routledge, 1992, p. 49.

24 D. d'Avray, *The Preaching of the Friars*, Oxford: Clarendon Press, 1985, p. 207.

25 Edwards, *op. cit.*, vol. 1, p. 217.

26 d'Avray, *op. cit.*, p. 45.

That was Humbert of Romans' aim in his *Treatise on Preaching*.[27] Humbert was the fifth Master-General of the Order of Preachers, holding the office from 1254 to 1263. It was still a novel view of a priestly vocation to hold, as Humbert did, that some (presumably the friars) were called to preaching as the central activity of their ministry.[28] Like Alan, Humbert offered his readers a series of ideas for sermons, but his preface to that is far more detailed than Alan's. Humbert explores how and why a man (Humbert refuses to entertain the possibility of a woman preaching)[29] might become a preacher, what he needs to exercise the office well, what the benefits of his ministry are, and various miscellanea which are involved in the preaching he envisages (such as the demands of itinerancy). It would appear that the treatise originally concluded with a selection of prayers for the use of preachers, but that this has been lost in the manuscript tradition.[30] Seen in its entirety, the treatise is not dissimilar to something that John Wesley might have constructed for the use of his preachers, and the editors of the 1955 Blackfriars translation of Humbert concluded that the work remains 'an excellent guide to fruitful preaching; may it also serve to enkindle the zeal of those who are chosen not only to offer the *Verbum Dei* on the altar but also to propound the *Verbum Dei* from the pulpit'.[31] That the contemporary relevance of the treatise is so easily recognized sets it apart from some of the later *artes praedicandi* which were very much products of their time.

The *artes* of the fourteenth century became increasingly schematized. It is a matter of some debate how far this was due to the influence of academic scholasticism,[32] but that detail is necessarily beyond the scope of this study. Humbert indicates the general trends that later writers were to continue; the similarities with the methods of Thomas Aquinas are obvious. Throughout the

27 S. Tugwell (ed.), *Early Dominicans: Selected Writings*, New York: Paulist Press, 1982, pp. 179–369.

28 Tugwell, *op. cit.*, p. 182.

29 Tugwell, *op. cit.*, p. 223.

30 Tugwell, *op. cit.*, p. 321.

31 *The Formation of Preachers*, p. vii.

32 d'Avray, *op. cit.*, p. 177.

treatise, Humbert's approach is to lay out the subject of discussion and then to break it down into smaller questions. His main theme – understanding the office of the preacher – is divided into seven topics, each of which is then subdivided into between three and ten subjects. The sermons that follow are also dependent on enumerating the issues, often, but not invariably, in three parts. After Humbert, division into three parts was to become a *sine qua non* of sermon structure. But that did not mean sermon structure was to be simple; far from it.

It is inadvisable to generalize too widely over a mass of literature, but it appears that the *artes praedicandi* of the fourteenth century recommended a common approach to the sermon. This does not seem to be the sermon (if there were one) that the laity would be offered at mass, but what those who had gathered to listen to a mendicant would hear. As with Alan, the starting point of the sermon structure (though not of the sermon itself) was the 'authority' or text. Robert of Basevorn, whose early fourteenth-century *Forma Praedicandi* (*The Form of Preaching*) can be taken as representative of the whole tradition,[33] makes his first point the 'invention' of the authority or 'theme'.[34] Once the preacher had announced the text, he would start somewhere away from it, with a protheme. This was part of the sermon that would draw the hearers into what followed (possibly in the expectation that the congregation would grow) by including some material related to the theme or to the occasion, and based on a second, related, biblical text. The protheme would end with the preacher asking the congregation to join with him in prayer for the preaching. Robert felt that it was important for there to be verbal links between the protheme and the prayer. The text or theme would then be announced again, and would be divided, usually into three parts. Robert cannot explain why the norm should always be three parts: 'either from respect to the Trinity, or because a threefold cord is not easily broken, or because this method is mostly followed by Bernard [of Clairvaux], or, as I

---

33 J. J. Murphy, *Three Rhetorical Arts*, Berkeley & Los Angeles: University of California Press, 1971, p. xx.

34 'Form of Preaching', tr. L. Krul in Murphy, *op. cit.*, p. 133.

think most likely, because it is more convenient for the set time of the sermon'.[35] Each part would then be sub-divided into (usually) three parts, and the sermon would proceed through the nine points, supporting each with illustrations (usually pious tales), quotations from the Church Fathers or from classical writers, and/or further biblical quotations; Robert outlined eight different methods of 'amplification' that could be used at this point.[36]

It is clear from Robert's work that balance was important in producing a well crafted sermon. One of Robert's 'ornaments' was 'correspondence', so that the 'first principal part is divided into *a b c*, the second into *d e f*, the third into *g h i* . . . there must be agreement among *a d g*, *b e h*, and *c f i*'.[37] Once the preacher had produced a well proportioned discussion of the theme, which needed, according to Robert, to persuade many 'to meritorious conduct',[38] and each section and the whole discussion had been carefully unified,[39] the sermon should then conclude with a prayer, which ideally should echo the opening of the sermon.[40] Following this advice, the preacher should be able to offer something that spoke clearly to the hearers and constituted a carefully crafted whole.

J. M. Neale believed that the norm in the Middle Ages was to preach extemporaneously and that the friars were able to do this for two reasons. One was that having an established form was itself an aid to memory; the other was that a thoroughgoing knowledge of Scripture underlay the preaching of this period.[41] Charles Smyth agreed that preaching according to this pattern drew widely on the Bible, but questioned how biblical it was.

> Such preaching may be extremely clever and ingenious, but its connection with the Word of God, though undeniable, is purely superficial and purely formal . . . The text from Scripture is

---

35 'Form of Preaching', p. 138.
36 'Form of Preaching', p. 180.
37 'Form of Preaching', p. 188.
38 'Form of Preaching', p. 120.
39 'Form of Preaching', pp. 196f.
40 'Form of Preaching', p. 200.
41 *Mediaeval Preachers and Mediaeval Preaching*, London, 1856, p. 8.

supposed to be the preacher's theme; it is in fact merely the peg on which he hangs a clever academic exercise.[42]

This was not expository preaching. The relationship of the text to the sermon was the reverse of what might be expected in modern times; Humbert makes this clear by outlining the content of a sermon and only suggesting a text (or a number of alternative texts) in the final paragraph of each example.[43]

Smyth's criticism (which echoes that of John Wycliffe)[44] rightly recognizes that this is not biblical preaching as other generations have understood that term, but the friars were doing far more than a clever academic exercise. What Smyth misses is the 'natural geography' of the mediaeval sermon form. This comes out nowhere more clearly than in the famous *arbor picta* of a sermon on the great commandments.[45] The manuscript of the *arbor* dates from the fifteenth century; it shows the protheme of the sermon (the lower trunk), the theme (Matthew 22.37–40), and the division of the theme into three branches (Why should we love God? Why should we love our neighbour? Why do all the Law and the Prophets hang on these two commandments?), each of which has three branches. Otto Dieter has convincingly argued that the originator of the tree was the late-thirteenth- or early fourteenth-century Dominican, Jacobus de Fusignano,[46] but whoever composed it, and whether or not it was unique at that time, the *arbor picta* graphically illustrates the way in which the minds of the writers of the *artes* were working. Theirs was not simply a linear approach to laying out their material. It was an organic view of preaching,[47] in which the subject matter grew out of a text for which the ground had been prepared through a protheme. They were using the 'natural geography' of the mind.

42 C. Smyth, *The Art of Preaching: A Practical Survey of Preaching in the Church of England (747–1939)*, London, 1940, p. 53.

43 Tugwell, *op. cit.*, pp. 326ff.

44 Smyth, *op. cit.*, pp. 53f.

45 In Munich Codex 23865; O. Dieter, 'Arbor Picta: The Medieval Tree of Preaching' in *The Quarterly Journal of Speech* 51 (1963), pp. 123–44.

46 Dieter, *op. cit.*

47 As Dieter notes, this is echoed in the approach of H. Grady Davis, *op. cit.*, p. 144. See below, pp. 72–8.

The idea of the mind's 'natural geography' has entered modern currency through the work of Tony and Barry Buzan, the creators of Mind Maps. Tony Buzan claims to have discovered a method of note-making and note-taking which uses a fuller range of the brain's ways of working than more traditional (linear) methods.[48] Over the last 20 or more years, the Buzans' work has become widely recognized world-wide and the idea of the mind map is a familiar one to millions of students and others. Their central argument is that the brain operates best when it uses all of its main skills (language, number, logic, rhythm, colour, imagery and spatial awareness) in combination with each other. They claim that the methods of taking notes and presenting material which are used by many communicators only use at most the first three of those skills, and usually only a very small part of the brain's potential within those three areas. So, for example, much academic communication depends on language but uses only that part of our language skill which is dependent on words and rarely ventures into the field of symbols. In order to make better use of the brain's capacity, those who follow the Buzan prescription are encouraged to think 'radiantly'. 'Radiant thinking . . . refers to associative thought processes that proceed from or connect to a central point.'[49] Mind Maps are the concrete expression of the brain's activity when people are taught that mental activity is multilateral rather than linear or one-dimensional. The mind mapper places the paper (and therefore represents visually the activity of their mind) in a landscape rather the portrait position, so that thoughts are laid out horizontally and in all directions, rather than vertically and downwards. From a central idea, thoughts radiate as branches, each thought itself becoming the subject of further associations, sometimes sub-dividing into other branches. The Buzans also argue that using a single pen and noting only words fails to recognize the different ways in which the brain makes connections. Mind mappers therefore organize their notes in different colours, with pictures or symbols as well as

---

48 Tony and Barry Buzan, *The Mind Map Book*, rev. edn, London: BBC Publications, 2003, pp. 48f.

49 *Mind Map Book*, p. 54.

words, and arrows and codes to show the connections that exist from one group of ideas to another.

Smyth's objection to the mendicant preachers of the Middle Ages fails to recognize that they seem to have been radiant thinkers. They focused on a single idea, which might be the occasion (a saint's day or whatever), the audience (for example, religious, lay, a guild), a virtue they wished to encourage or a vice they wished to discourage. From that single idea the rest of the sermon radiated. The system depended on what the mediaevals called 'distinctions'. A word or term would be treated under the different senses that it might have; so, for example, in a discussion of 'riches' a preacher (Guibert of Tournai) discussed 'temporal riches, spiritual riches, celestial riches and super-celestial riches'.[50] Similarly, the Buzan system depends on word association, as the thinker is encouraged to let the mind wander freely around the different meanings that a word might have and associated ideas which it may suggest.[51]

In selecting their text, the mediaeval preachers were encouraged to find one which would divide into at least three parts and then to ask questions of their texts. Often a sermon will revolve around why?, how?, what?, and so on. In the same way, the Buzans recommend the use of questions, particularly where association is not obvious.[52] Although the fourteenth-century writers (such as Robert of Basevorn) commended a threefold division wherever possible, earlier friars were not so prescriptive, and divisions into anything from two upwards are found in thirteenth-century sermons. However, the sacred or mystical numbers – three, four and seven – were the most popular devices, and it was rare for the number of subsections to exceed seven. The preaching friars from the thirteenth century onwards seem to have recognized something that the Buzans have also noted, that seven appears to be the number of items of information that a mind can hold.[53] 'In practice, therefore, the average

---

50 Quoted in d'Avray, *op. cit.*, pp. 173f.
51 *Mind Map Book*, pp. 59–64.
52 *Mind Map Book*, p. 97.
53 *Mind Map Book*, p. 94.

number of branches or Basic Ordering Ideas (BOIs) is between three and seven.'[54] Humbert was dismissive of preachers who tried to introduce too many divisions into their sermons, arguing that their efforts were counter-productive: 'a moderate amount of food is good for the stomach, but too much revolts it'.[55]

Figure 1 illustrates the content of a mediaeval sermon. The French Dominican William Peyraut preached (or at least wrote) his sermon on prayer some time in the second quarter of the thirteenth century.[56] His theme-text is 1 Peter 3.8: 'All be of one mind in prayer', though its relation to what follows is no more than superficial. The key term is prayer. Peyraut precedes his discussion with an introduction, a protheme (top centre of the plan) on a gloss on the Psalter on the centrality in righteousness of prayer, fasting and almsgiving. Having demonstrated the superiority of prayer to the other two disciplines, William is ready to tackle his main theme.

He divides his subject into two (making this what the Buzans would call a dyadic Mind Map). His main branches are why we should pray (shown on the right) and what Jesus taught about prayer (on the left). To the 'why' question, William offers six answers (on the right, moving from bottom to top). The first (that this is what Jesus taught) anticipates the second BOI (hence the arrow), and is itself divided into five sections (bottom middle). Again, William moves from bottom to top, dividing his last point (he taught us how we should pray) into four points, each supported by a biblical text. He then moves up his list of reasons to pray, developing the third into a threefold parallel to the protheme (prayer is easier than almsgiving or fasting), the fifth into a common ascending sequence of exemplars (the ordinary lay Christian, the saints, our Lord himself), and the sixth into a generalization about the main foci of human distress, again in three sections. In effect, there is a double meaning to each of these three sections, as the dangers are presented as both material and spiritual.

---

54 *Mind Map Book*, p. 117.
55 Tugwell, *op. cit.*, p. 206.
56 Tugwell, *op. cit.*, p. 165.

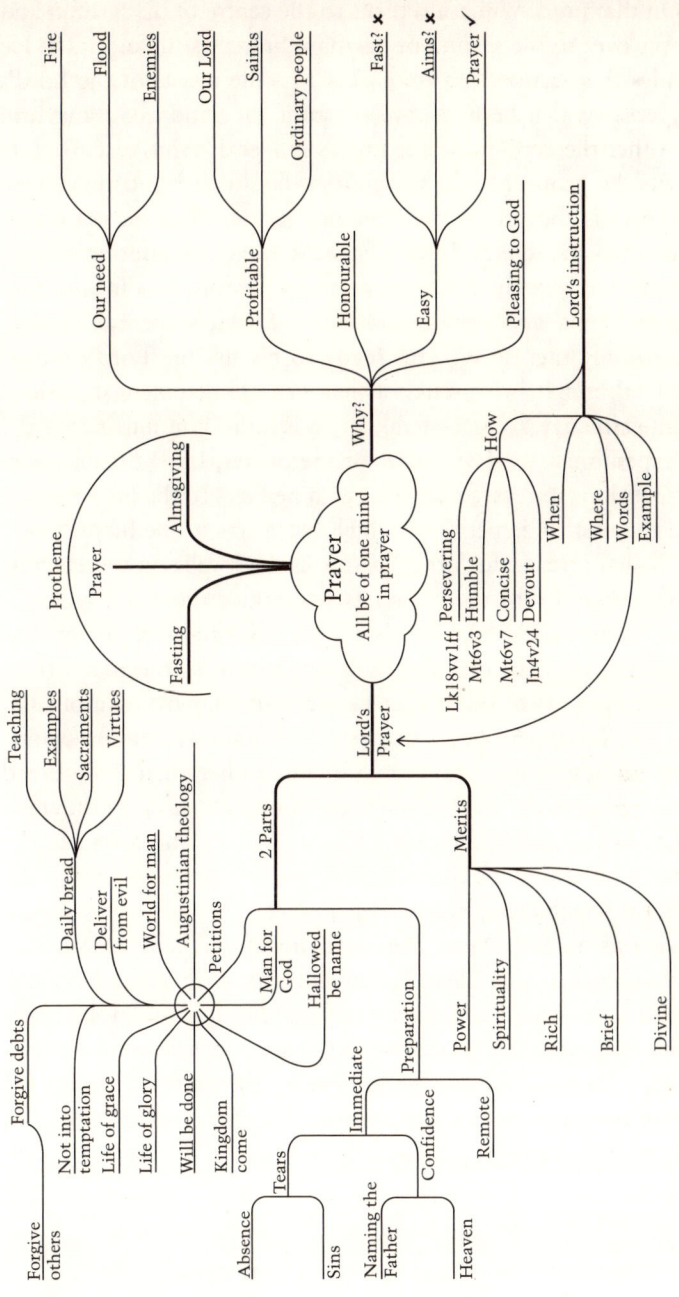

Figure 1. Mind Map of a Mediaeval Sermon

On that note, William returns to the centre of his sermon and moves over to the second of his main branches, Luke 11.1ff. He divides this section into two – the first the merits of the Lord's Prayer of which he finds five (bottom left hand quadrant) and the other the content of the Lord's Prayer. Having discussed its merits, he proposes that the content be divided into two parts. The first is the preparation for prayer, which again is divided into two – remote and immediate. Remote preparation can be disposed of quickly, but immediate preparation has (again) two aspects (tears and confidence) each of which operates in two ways. Only then is William ready to discuss the Lord's Prayer itself (although his discussion has been anticipated at various points already).[57] Once again, there is a division into two – the four petitions (the latter part of the prayer, but William treats the petitions in reverse order) which he links to the life of grace, and the first three petitions which he relates to the life of glory. As William treats the 'grace' petitions, he dwells on forgiveness, giving attention to the rider ('as we forgive those . . .') and on daily bread which, he reminds his hearers, can be of any of four types. Perhaps surprisingly, William finds that the move from the second part of the prayer to the first is far from automatic, and he takes us through a number of quotations from Augustine to show how those who are so low as to beg their daily bread can presume to think of the Kingdom of God. Each of the three petitions is briefly addressed, leaving William to complete the sermon by urging his congregation to yearn passionately for the holiness which is implied in their prayer.

Seen as a Mind Map, the structure of William's sermon (in all its complexity) is clear. Presumably, for a travelling preacher, such a structure would offer the flexibility not to develop fully some of the smaller branches of the sermon if time or circumstance called for brevity, or to develop the material more fully if a leisured approach were possible. William is unlikely to have had his text before him as he preached; the division and sub-

---

57 Links might be shown in the colour coding of a Mind Map.

division (which the Buzans call chunking) would have aided the recall in the memory.[58]

Some modern preachers, more accustomed to taking their notes into the pulpit, have embraced the Mind Map as a device for ease of reference when preaching. A single sheet is all that is needed for a mind-mapped sermon. That sheet is usually used with a landscape rather than portrait orientation. The vast majority of examples of Mind Maps which the Buzans offer indicate that this way of thinking naturally turns the paper horizontally rather than vertically (landscape rather than portrait), but that is not the only source of this sort of thinking in the world of homiletics. Peter Barber (in a revision to a Methodist training course)[59] recommended that preachers use radial thinking to do their exegesis, and Kenton Anderson proposes a non-linear approach to the story of the text on a quartered paper.[60] It would appear that increasingly preachers see the sermon not as following from the text or theme but revolving around it. A preacher who takes a Mind Map into the pulpit is using just such an approach.

Tony Buzan recommends that mind mappers take pride in their work with neatness and colour. Some Mind Maps have been displayed as works of art,[61] which is a curious development as the purpose of a Mind Map is to plan or to summarize a piece of work not to be a piece of work. That the plan should become an end in itself seems to have been an unintended, but not unwelcome, consequence of the Buzans' work, one which forms another unexpected parallel with the preaching of the mediaeval friars. By the end of the Middle Ages, there were those who believed that the message contained in a thematic sermon was in danger of being drowned by the elaborateness of its own structure. A carefully planned pattern to the preaching would attract the admiration of the auditors who

---

58 *Mind Map Book*, p. 94.

59 *Faith & Worship*, Unit One, Peterborough: Methodist Publishing House, 4th edn, 2003, pp. 28ff.

60 *Preaching with Conviction*, Grand Rapids: Kregel Publications, 2001, p. 68.

61 *Mind Map Book*, p. 107.

had heard many sermons in a similar form. An anonymous thirteenth-century preacher at St Victor in Paris complained that 'there are many, who, when they come to sermon . . . do not care what the preacher says; but only how he says it. And if the sermon be well "rhymed", if the theme be well "divided", if he pursues the argument well, if he "harmonizes" well . . . that is all they look for in the sermon.'[62] Forms tended, therefore, to become increasingly elaborate and, in the minds of some, unnecessarily so. As G. R. Owst rather elaborately summarized the problem, 'over-refinement and development of the homiletic armour now hampered or even suffocated its wearer, instead of equipping him the better for the battle'.[63] At the very time that 'the roots of Reformation were to be found in the late medieval preaching revival'[64] the humanists and the earliest reformers were beginning to suggest that there might be other, and better, ways of preaching.

In the mid-twentieth century, perhaps unwittingly, a leading homiletician was taking his students back to something close to the mediaeval practice. H. Grady Davis' 'design for a sermon' might be termed a modern *arbor picta*:[65]

A sermon should be like a tree.
It should be a living organism
With one sturdy thought like a single stem
With natural limbs reaching up into the light.[66]

In this design, Davis expressed the central idea of his approach to homiletics, that a sermon should be an organic whole. It was not to be structured according to any schema, but should be the natural development of a single thought.[67] Whether or not he

---

62 Quoted in G. R. Owst, *Preaching in Medieval England*, Cambridge, 1926, p. 312.

63 Owst, *op. cit.*, p. 308.

64 B. Kreitzer, 'The Lutheran Sermon', in L. Taylor (ed.), *Preachers and People in the Reformation and Early Modern Period*, Boston: Brill, 2001, p. 59.

65 Dieter, *op. cit.*, p. 143.

66 H. Grady Davis, *Design for Preaching*, Philadelphia: Fortress Press, 1958, p. 15.

67 Davis, *op. cit.*, p. 79.

recognized it, his image was one that had already been used in the Middle Ages. If the Buzan brothers are right, and it is important to take and to make notes using a wider range of forms and colours than many do, then the *arbor picta* (along with other forms of Mind Map) may again find its place in the pulpit in the early twenty-first century.

The teachers of classical rhetoric taught five disciplines. The second (which is the main focus here) was *dispositio* – the organization and arrangement of the speech. Before that came *inventio* – deciding what to say. The two cannot be completely divorced from each other – whilst orators or preachers are considering what their subject is, they may well already be considering how the finished article will be shaped. Mediaeval homileticians, like Humbert, could be scornful of preachers who chose a subject that did not lend itself to an elegant arrangement. Like the Mind Map, therefore, the *arbor picta* could be used both for note-making and for note-taking.

> It should have deep roots:
> As much unseen as above the ground
> Roots spreading as widely as its branches spread
> Roots deep underground
> In the soil of life's struggle
> In the subsoil of the eternal word.[68]

The first task of the preacher is to identify the theme (the trunk of the tree). This depends in part on where the tree has been planted (or what the occasion of the sermon is). In this example, the preacher is preparing to deliver a sermon on the anniversary of a church or the feast of its dedication. The roots which can be drawn onto the plan are in two parts. On the one side is the story of that congregation and its building. The preacher may be aware of the significant events of the past and of some of the hopes and fears for the future. On the other side are the appointed lections; in this case (for the purpose of example) Psalm 122; Genesis 28.10–22; 1 Peter 2.1–10; John 10.22–29.

---

68 Davis, *op. cit.*, p. 15.

If the preacher can visualize the sermon as a tree, the text is the point where the roots are just above the ground. One of the decisions that has to be made in the preparation is how much of the exegetical material needs to be brought to the surface. It may be that (with Humbert) the preacher wants to make this decision late in the process, finding from the lessons a single verse that expresses the core of the message that the preacher feels called to deliver. This core forms the theme of the sermon. In this case, the preacher has identified this as 'What it means to be the people of God' and takes as a text 1 Peter 2.9a: 'But you are a chosen race, a royal priesthood, a holy nation, God's own people.'

The text and theme having been identified, the preacher looks to 'dividing'. One possibility is to divide the text (and four 'branches' could emerge – chosen race, a royal priesthood, a holy nation, God's own people). In this case, however, the preacher believes this to be too restrictive and not to do justice to the poetic (and therefore repetitive) nature of Peter's thought. It is the theme that is to be divided, or rather (in Davis' terms) it is the central single idea of the sermon that needs to be developed. Davis maintained that the idea should have the form of a simple sentence[69] which in this instance could be 'God has chosen you to be in his Church'. However, in order that the branches of a tree might emerge, the trunk needs to have some girth, so the preacher will include in the sermon a discussion of the theme, exploring the idea of election and its biblical overtone of marital love with instances from the biblical narrative and the experience of Christians, including the sense that many in the congregation may have that their place among the privileged in the Church was not from their own choice but a response to the divine election. Once the theological understanding of election has been cogently and briefly (but not too briefly, as this is the trunk of the tree) expounded, the preacher can move to division.

> It should show nothing but its own unfolding parts;
> Branches that thrust out by the force of its inner life
> Sentences like leaves native to this very spray

---

69 *op. cit.*, pp. 34f.

True to the species
Not taken from alien growths.[70]

Election is a theme on which a great deal could be said but in the interests of clarity and brevity the preacher considers just three ideas and proposes that being a chosen people involves being chosen irrespective of our own merit, being chosen for a purpose (to listen to the shepherd's voice), and being chosen to receive a promised blessing. These ideas form the branches of the tree. Each can then be subdivided into an equal number of parts and in this case, again, that number is three. Bearing in mind Robert's stress on the value of 'correspondence', the preacher designs each of the three branches to have a biblical argument drawn from the appointed readings, an amplification (supported by illustration) of what this might mean to a Christian, and a point of application, which might suggest to the congregation some future action.

> Illustrations like blossoms opening from inside these very
>   twigs
> Not brightly coloured kites
> Pulled from the wind of somebody else's thought
> Entangled in these branches.
> It should bear flowers and fruit at the same time like the
>   orange
> Having something for food
> For immediate nourishment
> Having something for delight
> For present beauty and fragrance
> For the joy of hope
> For the harvest of a distant day.[71]

The first branch takes as its biblical base the comments of Peter ('Once you were not a people, but now you are God's people') and the story of Jacob. Jacob displayed reprehensible traits in his

---

70 *op. cit.*, p. 15.
71 *op. cit.*, p. 15.

dealings with his brother and was running away from the land and family of promise when God met him in the dream at Bethel. The Christian story is littered with examples of people called by God when apparently far from and travelling away from his grace which points to the truth that election is his gift and not dependent in any way on human merit. In the life of the church, therefore, there is no place for attitudes of superiority.

The second branch makes it clear that election does not come without responsibility. The theme of listening to the shepherd's voice develops ideas from John 10. Those who refuse to listen find themselves dissatisfied. The second 'twig' considers how we 'listen to the shepherd's voice' and supports this with stories of those who have been changed and who have changed the lives of others in response to what they have discerned Christ saying to them. The preacher completes this section by encouraging the congregation to engage with some form of Scripture study or devotional reading.

The third branch considers the blessing promised to the elect. This draws on both God's pledge to Jacob ('Your offspring shall be like the dust of the earth, and you shall spread abroad to the west and to the east and to the north and to the south; and all the families of the earth shall be blessed in you and in your off-spring') and on Jesus' words in the temple ('I give them eternal life, and they will never perish. No one will snatch them out of my hand.'). The preacher expounds the promise of which the Church is now a part and explores some of the tensions and difficulties that exist in the Church's life and which may appear to undermine the promise. The congregation are left with an exhortation to be thankful for present blessings and the assurance with which they face the future.

> To be all this it must grow in a warm climate
> In loam enriched by death
> In love like the all-seeing and all-cherishing sun
> In trust like the sleep sheltering night
> In pity like the rain.[72]

---

72 *op. cit.*, p. 16.

One part of the sermon remains to be included – the protheme. Humbert of Romans did not believe that a protheme was always necessary and it could be omitted here without any violence being done to the form of the sermon. On this occasion, the preacher feels it right to include one and takes (as a second text) the opening words of Psalm 122 ('I was glad when they said to me, "Let us go to the house of the LORD!"') which become the first line of the sermon. The preacher expresses gratitude for being appointed to preach this sermon and reflects on the joyfulness of the occasion. The mediaeval pattern may be adopted, of pausing with a brief prayer (perhaps asking that at this celebration those gathered may be enabled to enter more deeply into the source of their joy through words that bring life) before announcing for the second time the text from 1 Peter.

Inventio and *dispositio* may each leave the preacher with a picture of a tree. The latter might accompany the preacher into the pulpit, although in practice it might not be an easy tool to use. However, committed to memory in this visual form, it may help the preacher to deliver the sermon with cogency and perspicuity.

4

UNDERSTANDING, DOCTRINES AND USES

The Reformation Preaching of the Puritans

Those who study the structure of the sermon do so conscious that many others have trodden the path before them. In every age, even when one form of sermon may appear to dominate, some preachers will be varying their approach and some parts of the Church will be receiving their preaching in a different shape from that experienced in other places. In mid-seventeenth-century England there were at least five different patterns in common use, as is evidenced by Abraham Wright's *Five Sermons in Five Several Styles*. Wright's interest in the subject, he told his readers, had been prompted by the poor preaching of his own day. He therefore proposed to offer a number of creditable models for the instruction of struggling practitioners. His five sermons come from a variety of sources. Lancelot Andrewes provided the first example with a sermon to the royal court on Ash Wednesday, and Wright followed this with an ordination sermon by Bishop Hall. The University Sermon he included was attributed to 'Maine and Cartwright', but the authorship of the last two sermons is unclear. The fourth, and longest in the book (running to 91 pages out of a total of 236), is a Presbyterian sermon from

St Paul's Cathedral in London; the last (which Wright noted had never been preached) was an Independent sermon.

In two hundred years, these forms had come (to differing degrees and in different places) to supersede the thematic sermon of the friars. That change is one small aspect of a far greater transformation in not only the ecclesiastical but also the political life of Europe. It would be too simplistic to see Martin Luther setting in train a series of events when he nailed his theses to the door of the castle church in Wittenberg; the Reformation was a far more complex affair than that, originating from a number of causes, but All Hallows' Eve 1517 has a symbolism as the moment after which the seemingly inexorable tide of opposition to some parts of mediaeval catholic practice were to be given their head and allowed to splinter the Church, apparently irrevocably. Preaching was to play a leading part in the upheavals of the sixteenth and seventeenth centuries; it was to a preached message (the missions of the friars to sell indulgences) that Luther at first objected and throughout the Reformation controversies were worked out on both sides through sermons. For all that the recent invention of the printing press aided the Reformers, the Reformation was a preached Reformation as much as it was a printed Reformation, and it is possible to argue that the Reformation owed as much to the development of popular preaching in the fifteenth century as to the invention of the printing press, and the two belonged together.[1] The sermons of Luther, Zwingli, Calvin and others had an influence comparable to their books and pamphlets. It was also a Reformation in preaching. The ministry of the Word was never to be the same again, and for that printing was to a large degree responsible. Printers rushed onto the market the sermons of the influential preachers; the quantity of preaching that was published during the Reformation was enormous, though that reflects the fact that there was an enormous quantity of sermons being preached. Luther delivered over a hundred sermons in a

---

1 See, e.g., D. MacCulloch, *Reformation: Europe's House Divided 1490–1700*, London: Penguin, 2003, pp. 31–3.

year,[2] but that was only half of the number that Calvin was to offer in Geneva.[3] Heinrich Bullinger, Zwingli's successor at Zurich, left evidence of over 7,000 sermons from a 44-year ministry.[4] Objecting both to the style and content of the thematic sermons and to the paucity of preaching from many ordinary parish priests (and even some bishops) in the later Middle Ages, the Reformers aimed to restore both quality and quantity of preaching to the regular pastoral life of the Church.

Concerns about the quality or quantity of sermons did not feature in Luther's original protest. The Ninety-five Theses focused on the immediate cause for concern, the selling of indulgences. But underlying Luther's fury at what he perceived to be the cupidity and dishonesty of this practice lay a concern about the preaching ministry of the friars. One of the theses argued that 'They are the enemies of Christ and the pope who forbid altogether the preaching of the Word of God in some churches in order that indulgences may be preached in others.'[5] The pastoral role of preaching had been dislocated because of the activity of visitors. The restoration of the sermon to a central place in a priest's local ministry was to be one of the effects of the Reformation in both Protestant and Catholic churches. The indulgence dispute may have been the cause but it brought to light an undercurrent of discontent.

That discontent had had a continuing life in England since the Lollard movement was at its most powerful in the late fourteenth century. The Lollards had, in a number of respects, anticipated the changes of the Reformation, with their emphasis on the primacy of Scripture (and access to it in the vernacular), their rejection of some sacramental theology and their yearning for a return to what they saw as the simplicity of apostolic practice in the Church. The continuing influence of John Wycliffe (*c*. 1330–84) may not have been as great in fomenting religious

---

2 H. Bornkamm (tr. E. T. Bachmann), *Luther in Mid-career*, London: Darton, Longman and Todd, 1983, p. 199.

3 J. T. Ford, 'Preaching in the Reformed Tradition', in L. Taylor (ed.), *Preachers and People in the Reformation and Early Modern Period*, Boston: Brill, 2001, p. 65; MacCulloch, *op. cit.*, pp. 246f.

4 Ford, pp. 246f.

5 Thesis 53.

change in sixteenth-century England as historians used to argue (and as some scholars still maintain),[6] but (as in other respects) he had anticipated later changes with his attitude to preaching. Wycliffe scorned the complex thematic sermon, such as that detailed by another fourteenth-century Englishman, Robert of Basevorn, and adopted a simpler model, essentially seeing the task of the sermon as expounding the text and refuting error.[7] He was heavily influenced by Augustine, and Wycliffe's sermons are reminiscent of the fifth-century African in that they sometimes seem to conform to no previously recognized form. The sole criterion that mattered to Wycliffe was that a sermon should be plain and clearly understood.[8] Some early Wycliffe sermons are remarkably complex and demonstrate great flexibility in dealing with the biblical text; for example, preaching on John 19.27 ('Here is your mother'),[9] Wycliffe began by urging his congregation to take seriously their loyalty to the Church as their mother, but then went on with a discourse on the seven last words from the cross, which he presented (without complete consistency) as antidotes to the seven deadly sins. These in turn, he claimed, are reflected in the seven signs of death (for instance, *rigor mortis* is a symbol of pride which is contrasted with Jesus' humility 'Into your hands I commend my spirit'). Later, as he moved into opposition to the Church, Wycliffe returned to the patristic ('postil') model of verse-by-verse exegesis; for example, his sermon on the good wife of Proverbs 31 treats each clause in turn (though, still showing the influence of Augustine, in an allegorical manner as a symbol of the Church).[10] Wycliffe became increasingly impatient of thematic preaching, the prevalence of which he blamed on the friars. It is not always clear in Wycliffe's thought whether the friars were in error because they practised such preaching or whether such preaching was reprehensible because it came from

---

6 R. Rex, *The Lollards*, Basingstoke: Palgrave, 2002, pp. 143ff; cf. H. O. Old, *The Reading and Preaching of the Scriptures in the Worship of the Christian Church*, vol. 4, Grand Rapids: Wm Eerdmans, 2002, p. 136.

7 Wycliffe, *Sermones*, London: Wycliffe Society, 1887–90, vol. 1, p. xiii.

8 Wycliffe, *Sermones*, vol. 4, p. 268.

9 Wycliffe, *Sermones*, vol. 4, pp. 328–37.

10 Wycliffe, *Sermones*, vol. 4, pp. 147–51.

the mendicants. Wycliffe's hostility towards the Dominicans and Franciscans was unrestrained. They were 'the sons of Satan';[11] in his sermon on the evils of war, Wycliffe manages to reach the conclusion that the barrier to peace that most needed to be removed was the preaching of the friars.[12]

Wycliffe's opposition to the preaching of the friars was to be echoed by Desiderius Erasmus (1469–1536) at the beginning of the sixteenth century. Among the caustic passages in *In Praise of Folly*, the influential humanist scorned the sermons to which people were subjected.[13] The object of his satire was not so much the form as the content and style of the sermons; there were those who offered the most ridiculous analyses not of doctrine but of the symbolism of letters, there were preachers who indulged themselves in the most extraordinary histrionic displays and there were congregations who dozed through most sermons and paid attention only to the anecdotes which was all *exempla* had become. Erasmus' contribution to homiletics was not wholly negative, however. Towards the end of his life, he produced a massive work – *Ecclesiastes, sive Concionator evangelicus*. Like Augustine, Erasmus wanted to appropriate the art of rhetoric from antiquity in the service of the gospel. Preachers who knew how to construct and deliver a sermon would be more effective than those who strove merely to entertain their congregations or who struggled without training. Much depended on the character of the priest: 'it is the sincere disposition of the mind that prompts readiness of speech, an apposite delivery, and decent gestures'.[14] The art of rhetoric should be something that a preacher imbued but did not display. However, it could be learned, and Erasmus' aim was to provide the means whereby it might be. 'If elephants can be trained to dance, lions to play, and leopards to hunt, preachers can be taught to preach.'[15] A sermon,

---

11 Wycliffe, *Sermones*, vol. 4, p. 30.

12 Wycliffe, *Sermones*, vol. 4, p. 41.

13 *In Praise of Folly*, J. Wilson (tr.), London, 1668, pp. 115–21.

14 From the summary of *Ecclesiastes* in O. C. Edwards, *A History of Preaching*, vol. 2, Nashville: Abingdon Press, 2004, p. 238.

15 Quoted in R. Bainton, *Erasmus of Christendom*, London: Lion, 1988, p. 323.

therefore, like a classical oration, was most effective if composed in six parts – *exordium, narratio, divisio, confirmatio, confutatio* and *conclusio*,[16] each of which Erasmus studies and develops for the guidance of those who would be effective preachers.

This approach was very different from that of Martin Luther. Luther's contribution to the development of preaching was not by offering a distinctive shape (although his own sermons were unlike anything that had gone before)[17] but by raising its status. The sermon was no longer an optional extra in Lutheran worship; whenever the Church came together there should be preaching and prayer because it was preaching that defined the Church. For Luther, preaching was the Word of God alongside the Scriptures; a sermon was a moment in which, by faith, Christ came to the listener and the listener came to Christ.[18] No particular form was demanded for this experience; like Wycliffe, Luther appears to have been utterly idiosyncratic in the structuring of his sermons.[19] That there can be no certainty on this point is due to the peculiar nature of the sermons from Luther that exist in printed form. Most of these were published (sometimes without his permission and at other times from the 'official' notes of his amanuensis, George Rörer) in haste[20] after Luther's pulpit performances in which he preached from an outline from which he not infrequently departed.[21] The structure was often determined by two elements; the first, and more important, was Luther's desire to communicate the message of the Bible to the congregation. He rejected both the thematic sermon of the later Middle Ages and the older verse-by-verse expository model (even though he called his published collection a 'postil') in favour of a form that identified the core of a biblical passage

16 Edwards, *op. cit.*, vol. 2, p. 239.

17 Edwards, *op. cit.*, vol. 1, p. 295. For another view, see B. Kreitzer, 'The Lutheran Sermon', in L. Taylor (ed.), *Preachers and People in the Reformation and Early Modern Period*, Boston: Brill, 2001, p. 45.

18 R. Lischer (ed.), *The Company of Preachers: Wisdom on Preaching. Augustine to the Present*, Grand Rapids, Michigan and Cambridge, UK: Eerdmans, 2002, p. 115.

19 Edwards, *op. cit.*, vol. 1, p. 295.

20 Bornkamm, *op. cit.*, pp. 199f.

21 Edwards, *op. cit.*, vol. 1, p. 294.

and addressed that. The second consideration was the rebuttal of the objections of Luther's opponents, both Roman Catholics and the more extreme Protestants ('enthusiasts') whom he suspected of antinomianism.

An example of his distinctive manner of preaching is to be found in his sermon on the Good Shepherd.[22] He takes as his text John 10.11–16 and begins by stating that there are two forms of Christian preaching – that of law and that of gospel. As a Luther sermon seems not to be complete without an attack on the papacy, he adds to his opening comments that whereas both these forms of preaching are ordained by God, there is other preaching 'invented of men, ordained of the Pope and his prelates' whom he identifies with the thieves and robbers of John 10. The Good Shepherd is the chief preacher of the gospel and continues to be so after the ascension by putting his word into the hearts of his preachers.

Luther then turns his attention to Ezekiel's comments about the failed shepherds (Ezekiel 34.2–6). Their failure is in not caring for the weak and the excluded; the kingdom of heaven, Luther maintains, is open exclusively (like a hospital) to the weak and the outcast. This leads him to an evangelical appeal to any who feel themselves to be sinners to turn to Christ. He then moves to a discussion of those with whom Christ shares his ministry. At their best, they are also shepherds, who know their sheep and are prepared to share Christ's sufferings. Some, however, are hirelings, and they will abandon their posts or stop preaching in the face of persecution. The model of true ministry is Christ himself, and Luther expands on the self-giving of Christ in a moving passage in which he speaks as Jesus in the first person.

Then comes an abrupt switch. Jesus' words about others being gathered into the fold have been misinterpreted, Luther argues, as a promise of universal salvation. He takes them to apply to the mission to the gentiles. As there is no universal promise, the Church must continue to preach the gospel. And with that, Luther ends the sermon, as he typically does, with a prosaic clos-

---

22 M. Luther, *Sermons on the Most Interesting Doctrine of the Gospel*, London, 1830, pp. 69–80.

ing comment: 'thus much for a compendious exposition of the text'. Luther's method is simple; there are no rules of organization to be obeyed, just an identification of the key points of a text and a clarification of them in the face of error, at whatever length he deemed necessary.[23]

The Reformers in Switzerland took a different approach from Luther. Both Hulrich Zwingli and John Calvin returned to what they understood to be the patristic model of preaching and expounded the text verse by verse. Here the form of the sermon was dictated by theology as the object of the sermon was simply to make plain to the people the meaning of the Scripture that was being discussed. Both Calvin and Zwingli worked through the books of the Bible, week by week and sometimes day by day, much as John Chrysostom had done in Antioch. Neither preached from notes,[24] so the published sermons (like many of Luther's) were transcripts of what one of those present at the sermon had been able to take down. Zwingli's published sermons appear to have been heavily revised for publication,[25] but Calvin either did not have or did not make the time to do that revision. From 1549 onwards, the Genevan church employed a professional stenographer to take down Calvin's sermons in shorthand and to prepare them for publication. This could not have been an easy task; the first appointee had to devise his own system of shorthand and make notes with a quill pen whilst Calvin extemporaneously translated or paraphrased the text and spoke to it.[26] Calvin's comments on each verse or group of verses would usually be in two parts. In the first, he would expound the literal meaning and/or the doctrinal implication of the verse; in the second he would urge his audience to respond with appropriate Christian action. The structure of the sermon was determined by this pattern being repeated, with only a brief introduction (often merely doing no more than informing the congregation that he

---

23 Another of the remarkable features of Luther's preaching is the tremendous variation in length of the published sermons.

24 Ford, *op. cit.* p. 77.

25 Ford, *op. cit.* p. 78.

26 T. H. L. Parker, *Calvin's Preaching*, Edinburgh: Westminster John Knox Press, 1992, pp. 65ff.

would continue from the point he had reached in his last sermon) and a summary conclusion and call to prayer being added.

The crucial feature of a Calvin sermon was always its proximity to the text. Calvin's theology allowed for a high view of the act of preaching. The Bible was God's message to humankind, and the task of the preacher was to relay that message to his own generation. Whilst Calvin did not believe that a sermon was the Word of God in the same way as the Bible ('the permanent form of God's truth'),[27] the message of the preacher was the same message as that of the Bible, but delivered through the agency of an additional messenger.[28] It was a task which demanded on the part of the preacher the utmost seriousness and from the congregation the utmost respect.

Calvin's sermons were translated into English and became very popular among British Protestants. His method of 'doctrine and use' was the basis for a number of preaching manuals of the sixteenth century, one of which was the influential *Arte of Prophesying* by William Perkins. By the time of Perkins' work, Reformation theology in England had developed three distinct strands of thinking about preaching, which in places were mutually exclusive. The first strand viewed it with far less enthusiasm than did Luther, Zwingli or Calvin, and is represented by (among others) Richard Hooker (1554–1600). Hooker was himself highly respected as a preacher, exercising his ministry as Master of the Temple Church in London from 1584 to 1592. There he was engaged in an extraordinary competition for the minds of his hearers with the Reader at the church, William Travers. 'Canterbury in the morning and Geneva in the afternoon' was the diet for those who attended worship there.[29] In this controversy, 'the great debate of the English Reformation' was rehearsed.[30] It may have been the debilitating effect of Travers' continual opposition or it may have

---

27 *Institutes* I, 7 (quoted in Parker, *op. cit.* p. 2).

28 Parker, *op. cit.*, pp. 23f.

29 More accurately, 'The forenoon sermon spake Canterbury and the afternoon Geneva' (Isaac Walton, quoted in McAdoo, 'Richard Hooker', in G. Rowell (ed.), *The English Religious Tradition and the Genius of Anglicanism*, Oxford: Ikon, 1992, p. 109).

30 P. Secor, *The Sermons of Richard Hooker*, London: SPCK, 2001, p. viii.

been his philosophical understanding of the role of the State in the life of the Church that led Hooker to support the Elizabethan government's policy of limiting the number of sermons preached. After the traumatic years of Edward and Mary, Elizabeth I was all too aware of the inflammatory power of preached theology, and she wished to curtail the activities of extreme Protestants. Preaching was therefore restricted to those who were licensed by their bishops (a privilege that was not granted automatically to parish priests) and bishops were encouraged to be conservative in the number of licences they issued.[31] The explanation for Hooker's approach may also have been the influence of the Zwinglian Reformer Bullinger, as Parker suggests.[32] Such was the high view of Scripture that Bullinger took, those who followed him could (against the understanding of Luther and Calvin) see preaching as non-essential to worship. Whatever the process of thought, Hooker's position was that preaching was beneficial to the Church, but that what was of greater blessing was the unadorned reading of the Scriptures. Here he gave theological grounding to the Book of Common Prayer whose offices had no place for a sermon and with which were published the authorized homilies which ministers were instructed to read in place of their own material.

The second strand of English preaching followed the line set out by, among others, Erasmus, who Susan Wabuda argues was the greatest influence on preaching in sixteenth-century England, in moving preachers away from the thematic sermon into a type of preaching that was at once both classical, in that it drew on Ciceronian oratory, and personal, in that it depended on a view of the preacher as a vessel of divine activity.[33] Philipp Melanchthon, the disciple of Luther, whose approach was extremely influential in the second generation of the Lutheran Reformation,[34] can also be credited with shaping preaching in England. Melanchthon's great strength was as a student of classical rhetoric (he was not

---

31 Horton Davies, *Worship & Theology*, vol. 1, *From Cranmer to Hooker*, Princeton: Princeton University Press, 1970, p. 231.

32 Parker, *op. cit.*, p. 20.

33 S. Wabuda, *Preaching during the English Reformation*, Cambridge: Cambridge University Press, 2002, pp. 68ff.

34 Edwards, *op. cit.*, vol. 1, pp. 299f.

himself a preacher).[35] In England, this tradition of rhetorical preaching was to find its voice in the 'high church' Anglicanism of the early Stuart period. Lancelot Andrewes (1555–1626) is usually taken to be the representative of this school. Andrewes served as Bishop of Chichester, then Ely, and then Winchester. He was a favourite of Kings James I and Charles I and preached for the royal court on the great festivals and other important occasions. His reputation as a preacher was considerable, as his sermons before the king were deliberately produced to be works of literary merit. He combined the arts of rhetoric with an easy affinity with patristic authorities and a colourful use of language which delighted his audience;[36] he mastered his intellectual argument, but also aimed to appeal to the emotion of his listeners. His aim (which was shared by others such as John Donne (1571–1631) and, although he tended to a sparser, 'Senecan', rhetoric, Jeremy Taylor (1613–67)) was so to use language and imagery that something of the glory and mystery of God was revealed in the magnificence of the sermon.[37]

The third strand in English Reformation preaching can be understood as a reaction to the other two. Against the Erastian suspicion of preaching, the Puritans emphasized its indispensability to an act of worship; against the Erasmian dependence on the ornamentations of rhetoric, the Puritans looked to develop a 'plain style'. John Hooper, who was Bishop of Gloucester during the reign of Edward VI, seems to have pioneered this style (having been influenced by the practice in Zurich).[38] Despite the periods when there were attempts to suppress Puritan preaching, the method thrived and was developed in a number of text books. The most influential of these was William Perkins' *The Arte of Prophesying*, which was published in Latin in 1592 and translated into English in 1606. Perkins was influenced by the logic of the French philosopher Pierre de la Ramée, whose

---

35 Kreitzer, 'The Lutheran Sermon', p. 49.

36 Horton Davies, *Worship & Theology in England* vol. 2: *From Andrewes to Baxter and Fox*, Princeton: Princeton University Press, 1975, pp. 144f.

37 Davies, *op. cit.*, vol. 1: *From Cranmer to Hooker*, Princeton, 1970, pp. 157ff.

38 Davies, *op. cit.*, vol. 1, pp. 304f.

practice was almost invariably to express his thought through twinned ideas.[39] So, for Perkins, the task of a Christian minister is twofold (to preach and to pray), the values of preaching are twofold (to gather the elect and to drive away wolves), there are two matters of importance about preaching (preparation and performance) and so forth. This is symptomatic of an underlying Puritan theology that bordered on the dualistic, with a strong concern to strengthen the elect (and to dismiss the claims of those who clearly were not 'godly').

Perkins' discussion continued to develop his twofold approach. A text should be chosen and its meaning discerned – either plain or hidden. A hidden meaning is one which needed to be sought out by the preacher because the plain meaning was contradictory to something else in the Bible. Once the meaning was established, the preacher divided the text, which meant both resolving it (expounding the doctrine implicit in the passage) and applying it (enabling the congregation to see the implication of the doctrine for them and their situation). This application could be theoretical (in that the preacher might be aiming to refute error or to clarify misunderstandings) or practical (in that listeners might need to be persuaded to change their behaviour in response to what they heard). From this essentially binary system (rather like a computer programmer) Perkins produced a remarkably complex structure for his typical sermon. For a text from Matthew 10, he argued that it was possible to discern six doctrines which themselves led to thirteen uses. Six of these were in the form of mental application; those of practical application were further subdivided into three (positive) instructions and four (negative) corrections. The preacher might not use all this material, and indeed should not. Having determined what the content of his sermon might be, the minister needed to consider six possible categories of listener (from the ignorant and unteachable to believers eager to learn more) and the probability that the auditory would not be homogeneous.[40]

---

39 William Perkins (ed. S. B. Ferguson), *The Art of Prophesying with the Calling of the Ministry*, Edinburgh: Banner of Truth Trust, 1996, p. xii.

40 Perkins, *op. cit.*, pp. 66ff.

Given the complexity of this approach, it is not surprising that Puritan sermons were lengthy. How long is a matter of some uncertainty, although it is not unlikely that an hour was seen as brevity and three times that not uncommon, but long sermons were far from rare among other ecclesiastical parties in the seventeenth century.[41] However, it is probably no coincidence that Wright's 'Sermon in Presbyterian Style' is by far the longest of the five. For the dedicated Puritan seeker, such length was no disincentive. Many of the Puritan congregations were self-selecting and came in search of meaty fare. There was a conscious yearning for sound doctrine, and dissenters in particular would align themselves to one with a reputation for 'searching, convincing and lively ministry'.[42] The taking of notes during sermons was common practice as was discussion of the sermon (with or without the preacher) during the week following.

A late example of Puritan preaching is the ministry of Stephen Charnock (1628–80). Charnock is not a familiar name today, but in the seventeenth century he was widely known and respected as a writer and preacher. As with many Puritan writers, the relationship between the preaching and the published writing is sometimes less than straightforward, as it was a common practice to expand sermon material in order for it to be published as a 'Discourse' or 'Treatise'. The body of work surviving from Charnock is severely limited also by the facts that much of his manuscript remains (along with his beloved library) was destroyed in the 1666 Fire of London and that his publishing was curtailed by the years that he spent in the politico-ecclesiastical wilderness during the reign of Charles II. His early career had been promising; a protégé of Archbishop Sancroft, he was a minister in Southwark and a Fellow of New College, Oxford, during the years of the Civil War. Like many of the most gifted of the Puritans, Charnock was closely associated with the Commonwealth regime of Oliver Cromwell, and served from 1656 as chaplain to

---

41 G. R. Cragg, *Puritanism in the Great Persecution*, Cambridge: Cambridge University Press, 1957, pp. 213f.

42 Cragg, *op. cit.*, p. 203.

the Governor of Ireland, the Lord Protector's son, Henry.[43] After the Restoration, Charnock was (not surprisingly) out of favour with the new regime and was unable to find an appointment for 15 years (which time he appears to have spent travelling), before he was appointed as a second minister to the Independent Congregation in Crosby Square, a post he held until his death.[44] Given all these restrictions, the body of work that the student of Charnock has to study is limited, but there are extant publications (mainly transcribed from surviving sermon notes) which enable us to examine the structure of his preaching. The reason for Charnock's popularity in his own age and the value of his sermonic material to the modern student are to do with the weight of the ideas that he asked the form to carry. The Puritan sermon was primarily a vehicle for the imparting of sound doctrine to the elect. As for Calvin, the line for a seventeenth-century Puritan between a sermon and a lecture was thin and easily crossed; 'many sermons were really lectures'[45] and the preaching appointments which the wealthier Puritans funded in order to counter the anti-preaching bias of the Erastians (such as that which was, ironically, to cause such trouble to Charles Simeon)[46] were usually called 'lectureships'. Charnock never spared his listeners theological detail, and while some apparently praised his 'perspicuous plainness, convincing cogency, great wisdom, fearless honesty, and affectionate earnestness',[47] others found him 'too high for the vulgar hearers' and 'perhaps better suited to the more intelligent sort of Christian'.[48] A Charnock sermon is no more easy reading than it was easy listening, but it provides a clear and practical model for the way in which Puritan preaching wrestled with doctrine and attempted to apply it to the people who the preacher believed were called to godliness.

43 W. Symington, *Life and Character of Charnock*, Fire and Ice Publications, 1846, p. 4.

44 Symington, *op. cit.*, pp. 5f.

45 Cragg, *op. cit.*, p. 210.

46 See below, p. 112.

47 Symington, *op. cit.*, p. 12.

48 Cragg, *op. cit.*, p. 215.

An example of the detail with which Charnock treated the biblical text is shown by his *Discourse on the Pardon of Sin*. This is a long and complicated sermon on a text from Psalm 32 – 'Blessed is he whose transgression is forgiven, whose sin is covered. Blessed is the man unto whom the Lord imputes not iniquity.' Charnock begins with an exegetical introduction, suggesting that the psalm was written by David after his adultery with Bathsheba and was used liturgically in the Old Testament temple. He then draws his audience's attention to seven words and displays his considerable Hebrew scholarship. The meaning of the first word, 'blessed', is to be understood in the context of three which refer to human sinfulness ('transgression', 'sin' and 'iniquity') and three which describe God's pardon ('forgiven', 'covered' and 'imputes [not]'). Charnock notes, but only notes, that the three words for sin used here are also used in Exodus 34 when God discloses his name to Moses. His brevity here suggests that the published sermon is shorter than the oral event would have been.

Charnock then lays out the division of his subject, which he proposes to treat in five sections. The first is 'the nature of pardon'. He discusses the implication of the three words used (confusingly rendering two of them as 'covered') and offers some thoughts on how this might be misunderstood. The second section describes the author of pardon, and argues that pardon is the action of God operating out of his prerogative, his mercy, his justice, and his power. Charnock then moves on to discuss what is involved in forgiveness, both in terms of what God has done in Christ to pardon sinners and what sinners need do by faith to become the beneficiaries of God's mercy. The fourth section is a discussion of the extent of mercy and what it means to talk about God's perfect forgiveness and the fifth part argues that blessedness is the end result of being pardoned and what this means.

That is the first half of the sermon, which is essentially the doctrine, although (as is shown below) there are elements of application included. Charnock now moves to the 'uses' or direct application to his hearers. Again, there are five of these.

The first describes the misery that results from not accepting God's forgiveness. The second offers comfort to those in need of pardon by describing more of its benefits. The third 'use' asks the congregation to consider whether or not they have been pardoned, analyses errors that lead those not forgiven to believe themselves so and *vice-versa,* and describes the character of a forgiven person. The last two 'uses' are exhortation, firstly to those who are not pardoned (a category subdivided into those who don't care and those who do) and then to those who are sure that they are forgiven. The sermon ends abruptly as those in this last group are urged to contentment.

The structure of this sermon (and its adherence to the Perkins model) can be shown if it is reduced to a skeleton:–

Text	Psalm 32.1f.
Understanding	Blessed/blessedness
	Three words which describe sin
	Three words which describe forgiveness
Doctrine I	The nature of forgiveness
	• as 'covering' or blotting out
	• four implications of this doctrine
	• as 'covering' or drowning
	• four implications of this doctrine
	• as 'not imputing'
	• two implications of this doctrine
Mental Applications (correcting errors)	Existence of sin *is not* taken away
	Nature of sin *is not* taken away
	Demerit of sin *is not* taken away
	Guilt of sin *is* taken away
Doctrine II	The Author of forgiveness
	The act of God
	The prerogative of God
	• as proprietor
	• as sovereign
	• as governor

	• from mercy, unrelated to human merits
	The tender mercy of God
	• against his other attributes
	• unconstrained
	• resolved and designed
	• delightful and pleasant
	The justice of God
	The power of God
Doctrine III	How forgiveness is carried out
	God's action in Christ
	• Christ's death
	○ commanded by the Father
	○ willingly accepted by the Son
	• Christ's resurrection
Mental Application (the content of faith)	Human faith in
	• God's willingness to pardon
	• the certainty of forgiveness
	• the extent of forgiveness
	• continuing forgiveness
	• the value of forgiveness
Doctrine IV	The extensiveness of forgiveness (its perfection)
	• a perfect act
	necessarily so
	○ because all God's action is perfect
	○ because it is for God's glory
	• perfect in effect
	○ regardless of the quality of human wickedness
	○ regardless of the quantity of sins
	○ enduring
Doctrine V	The effect of forgiveness – blessedness
	• sin is taken away
	• blessings are conferred
	○ the favour of God

- access to God
- peace of conscience
- thankful heart ('all mercies are sweetened')
- endurance ('all afflictions are sweetened')

Use I	The misery of not being pardoned
Mental Application	• there is no middle way • to refuse pardon is to refuse God's other blessings • the need for pardon is increasing • God will be our judge at the last
Use II	The comfort of being pardoned
Mental Application	• it is a permanent state • the pardoned cannot be accused • the pardoned will be justified at the last • even little faith can be rewarded with pardon
Use III	Examination
Practical Application	• the importance of Christians examining their own state

Mental Application	• refutation of reasons the unpardoned believe themselves pardoned
	  ○ minor sins still incur God's wrath
	  ○ a few sins still incur God's wrath
	  ○ common sins still incur God's wrath
	  ○ that God has not (yet) punished does not indicate pardon
	  ○ prosperity does not indicate pardon
	  ○ forgetting sins does not indicate pardon
	  ○ hoping for mercy does not indicate pardon

- refutation of reasons the pardoned
  believe themselves not pardoned
  - afflictions
  - terror of conscience
  - sense of sin
  - remainder of sin

Practical Application
- Signs of a pardoned person
  - sincerity
  - sorrow for sin
  - fear of sin
  - sanctification
  - forgiving others
  - loving God

Use IV   Exhortation

Practical Application
- Those careless of their own state
  should seek forgiveness
  - earnestly
  - now
- Those longing for forgiveness need
  - to believe in the willingness of God
    to forgive
  - to believe in the capacity of God to
    forgive
  - to be humble
  - to plead God's glory

Use V   Exhortation

Practical Application
- Those who are forgiven should
  - admire God's grace
  - continue to serve God
  - continue to avoid sin
  - be content with their lot

There is no conclusion; it may be that Charnock (like Zwingli
and Calvin) moved from his last point into a prayer that picked

up the themes of the sermon, it may be that in the oral delivery there was some other form of peroration that was not included in the published version, or it may be that having arrived triumphantly back at the point from which he started (his text from Psalm 32), Charnock sat down. Despite its considerable length, there is nothing in this sermon that is not crucial to Charnock's argument. This sermon form was not designed to be elegant (although the best of Puritan preaching was not, apparently, unattractive); it was designed to be a vehicle for doctrine in an era in which theological arguments were hotly contested, and (in the hands of Charnock or one of his peers) it had to carry a great deal. To a Puritan convinced that the calling of the preacher was to form a godly people, a task which could only be achieved through the articulation of sound doctrine, the substantial and well organized sermon of this sort was a necessary vehicle.

The worshipper of the early twenty-first century might well find listening to such a substantial sermon an unfamiliar experience. Some feel that the difference between preaching in Charnock's day and ours is too great and that the conciseness of modern preaching is itself a problem. 'Sermonettes', complained Michael Green, 'make Christianettes.'[49] His objection was to the lack of content as well as the brevity of many late twentieth-century sermons and, while up to a point there can be both concision and profundity, the two features are closely connected. Some evangelical churches in Britain in the twenty-first century may still attract a following for a lengthy sermon but in most mainstream denominations 20 minutes appears to be the upper limit of what is tolerable to the congregation. There have been those who have argued that even that is too much. In a society in which time is of the essence and people have access to 24-hour news coverage in which things happen at remarkable speed, and human consciousness is dominated by visual and broadcast media, attention spans have lessened so that, some say, it is unreasonable to expect any but the most gifted of orators to hold an 'ordinary' congregation for more than eight to ten minutes. The effect of

---

49 J. Stott, *I Believe in Preaching*, London: Hodder and Stoughton, 1982, p. 7.

the liturgical movement in Anglican and Methodist churches (among others) has also contributed to a setting of the sermon within worship which tends to restrict its length.

However, there are occasions when a more discursive approach is required and where the sermon has a dominating position in the service. Some churches will have an event or a series of events in which the sermon is removed from any regular liturgical context and given an hour or so to itself. These are not lectures, although there is something of a parallel with the mid-week lectures which the Puritans offered in addition to Sunday worship. The expectation is that the content should be devotional rather than academic, they are not the occasions for questioning the speaker and they are usually set in a worship context, preceded by a hymn and prayer and followed by a blessing. Those who attend such 'talks' are usually regular churchgoers who value the extended treatment of matters of faith and practice which these occasions provide. For the speaker (sometimes a minister in local pastoral charge and sometimes a guest with a particular range of interest) this sort of event provides an opportunity to develop a subject at greater length than usual; the Puritan method of 'doctrines and uses' can provide a suitable pattern.

In this example, a speaker has been invited to contribute to a series of Lenten addresses in a city centre church. The theme of the series is simply 'The Cross' and the organizer wants those attending to be enabled to reflect on why the symbol of a cross has a central place in most church buildings. The preacher in this case reflects on 'The Cross that we carry' and takes as a text Matthew 16.24, Jesus' instruction that those who would be his disciples must deny themselves, take up their cross and go after him. There are three doctrinal points that the preacher wishes to develop. The first is the scandal of the cross, both in the social understanding of the Roman Empire and in the theological viewpoint of the Old Testament. This asks questions of the way that the symbol of the cross is used in the church and by modern Christians. The second is that the disciple's cross is a sharing in the saving work of Christ. This is a difficult idea and needs some mental application to address possible misunderstandings. The third point argues that to share in Christ's work in this way is a gift of grace, for which the Christian needs to pray and to be prepared to see opportunities. In the final section, the preacher wants to offer some practical suggestions ('Uses') to the congregation as they focus on the devotional aspects of the season of Lent. As in the Charnock example, the number of uses balances the number of doctrines and the second part of the sermon picks up the ideas of the first and reinforces them. As a skeleton, the sermon might look something like this:

Text	Matthew 16.24: Then Jesus told his disciples, 'If any want to become my followers, let them deny themselves and take up their cross and follow me.'
Introduction	Announcing the three headings of the doctrines to assist the congregation in following the argument
Doctrine I	The scandal of the cross • crucifixion the lowest form of punishment in the Roman Empire, reserved for slaves and rebels and not a subject for polite conversation • Old Testament understanding of the hanged man as cursed by God (references to Galatians 3.13 and Deuteronomy 21.23)
Application	How do we view the symbol of the cross? • as an item of jewellery? • as a necessary (unnoticed?) sign in/on a church? • as a gesture to mark our prayers (so others might see)? None of these recognizes the horror of the idea of carrying the cross

Doctrine II	The cross we carry is part of Christ's saving work. Discussion of Colossians 1.24 (in which Paul talks about his suffering 'completing what is lacking in Christ's afflictions')
Application (correcting errors)	This does not mean that Christ's work was not 'full, perfect, and sufficient' Cross-carrying is the way in which the Church (the Body of Christ) identifies fully with its Lord and pleads his case
Doctrine III	To carry the cross is a gift of grace. The 'privilege' accorded to Simon of Cyrene (Matthew 27.32), who may (given the identification of him in Mark) have become a disciple
Use I	We must pray for grace to endure humiliation (Heb 13.13: 'Let us go to him outside the camp') • Christian discipleship has nothing to do with social respectability • Christian discipleship has nothing to do with religious respectability
Use II	We must pray for opportunities to share Christ's humiliation • the acceptance of a low state witnesses to Christ's way
Use III	We must look for opportunities to share Christ's humiliation • how can a twenty-first western Christian identify with the despised of society?

Conclusion   Repetition of the text
                                  The cross has a central place as a symbol
                                  of Christ's glory and our calling
                                  There is no other way that Jesus offers

This is not a form that can be preached easily. It requires a considerable amount of concentration on the part of both preacher and listeners. But it has advantages for those occasions when a more detailed presentation than most Sunday sermons is required. By moving in different ways from doctrine to use, by varying the types of use, and by ending with a series of uses, the method invites the congregation to apply to their contemporary existence that which they are learning from the exposition of the Scriptures. What initially seems abstruse can offer practical Christianity (which is precisely what the seventeenth-century Puritans aimed to do).

5

CLASSICAL EVANGELICAL PREACHING

The Contribution of Charles Simeon

Among historians of preaching there is common agreement that in late seventeenth- and early eighteenth-century England John Tillotson (1630–94) was the doyen of preachers. According to a contemporary, 'he was not only the best Preacher of the age but seemed to have brought Preaching to perfection'.[1] It is a curious comment on the national church that it is also agreed that he is alone among Augustine's successors in enjoying 'the reputation for being the greatest preacher of his day'.[2] Not only were his sermons well attended, they were widely circulated, read both in the drawing room as literature and in churches as part of worship; that paragon of clerical idleness, James Woodforde, quite openly preached them from his own pulpit, though in an abbreviated version.[3] Tillotson's widow is reported to have been asked to sell the copyright to his sermons for £2,000.[4] However, those

---

1 G. Burnett, *History of His Own Time* (1724), quoted in W. F. Mitchell, *English Pulpit Oratory from Andrewes to Tillotson*, London, 1932, p. 337.

2 C. Smyth, *The Art of Preaching: A Practical Survey of Preaching in the Church of England 747–1939*, London, 1940, p. 103.

3 Smyth, *op. cit.*, pp. 153, 158.

4 J. Downey, *The Eighteenth-Century Pulpit*, Oxford: Clarendon Press, 1969, p. 24.

who have studied Tillotson in more recent years have failed to agree on what it was that made his preaching so attractive. 'It is hard for ordinary people of today to understand how it could have been so popular at the time. It is even hard for specialists who have studied it to understand its appeal.'[5]

Tillotson's importance in the history of homiletics is symbolic. He was the prime example of a style of preaching that was a reaction against what had gone before, both in the lengthy and complex sermons of the Puritans (like Charnock) and the baroque elaborations of the metaphysicals (like Andrewes). But he was not an originator; his method was largely dependent on the teaching of his father-in-law, John Wilkins (1614–72). Wilkins had published a short treatise in 1646 under the title *Ecclesiastes, or a Discourse concerning the Gift of Preaching as it Fals under the Rules of Art*, the aim of which was to make preaching both 'easier for the preacher and more profitable for the hearer'.[6] A sermon, according to Wilkins, had to achieve three ends: to teach clearly, to convince strongly, and to persuade powerfully. This gave the sermon a simple three part structure:

* explication (in which a text was analysed or a doctrine examined),
* confirmation (in which positive proofs of the thinking were advanced and/ or objections to it dismissed)
* application (which might be doctrinal or practical).

For Wilkins, the essence of a sermon was propositional. *Exempla* were to be kept to a minimum, lest they distract from the preacher's argument.

One of the reasons for the admiration that Tillotson attracted was the clarity of his structure. His later lack of popularity was due less to the manner of his addresses than to what he said. Tillotson was one of the first leaders of the Latitudinarians. Coming from Puritan stock and having lived through the religious and political upheavals of the Civil War, Tillotson spoke for many

---

5 O. C. Edwards, *A History of Preaching*, vol. 1, Nashville: Abingdon Press, 2004, p. 413.

6 *Ecclesiastes*, p. 1.

who were looking for a more irenic approach to matters of faith. The influence of the Cambridge Platonists had moved him to a more moderate position, although he was implacably opposed to James II's plans for the accommodation of Roman Catholicism (the anti-Catholic passages in his sermons being anything but irenic). His tolerant attitude led to doubts being voiced in later generations about his orthodoxy, but Tillotson was no Deist. A fairer objection was that under Tillotson the message of the gospel was reduced to a rational approach to life, and the mission of the Church made equivalent to that of a society for the reformation of manners. Tillotson was never prepared to suggest anything in a sermon that could not be supported with the evidence of reason, though that did not mean that he rejected the value of revelation (as his sermon on the possibility of the Resurrection demonstrates).[7] That may have been part of the reason for his popularity; in the eyes of some of the next generation, it was his greatest weakness. Charles Smyth quotes Canon Overton: 'Beyond a general impression that it is more prudent on the whole to believe the Gospel . . . than not, what impression does Tillotson convey?'[8]

The justice of that comment can be borne out in the reading of some of Tillotson's sermons. 'The Christian Life, a Life of Faith' serves as an example.[9] It also demonstrates the Wilkins form of explication, confirmation, application. Tillotson begins by discussing the background to his text, 2 Corinthians 5.7. In the midst of his sufferings, Paul had expressed confidence that all ultimately would be well. Tillotson identifies the reason for this confidence in the parenthesis – 'we walk by faith, not by sight'. Faith ('the firm persuasion and expectation of a thing') rather than sight ('the [present] possession and enjoyment') is the governing principle of Christian life. From this explanation, Tillotson makes three observations by way of confirmation (presenting them in summary at the end of the explication).

---

7 Sermon 193 (John Tillotson, *Works*, vol. 8, London: Richard Priestley, 1820, pp. 327–44).

8 Smyth, *op. cit.*, p. 162.

9 Sermon 83 (*Works*, vol. 4, pp. 184–200).

Tillotson's rationalism shines through the three sections of his discussion. Firstly, he states that Christians have good reason for faith, because they have been advised of the blessings of heaven and the pains of hell. Next, he explores what he takes to be a truism that 'faith is a degree of assent inferior to that of sense'. He proves this by scriptural references (1 Cor. 13.9f., 12) and the theological understanding that faith is temporal; more, he goes on to demonstrate that it is better that we do not know indubitably what our eternal fate is as such knowledge would be too great for us and it would be unreasonable for us, as it would make faith a necessity not a virtue, effectively removing (though Tillotson does not use the phrase) a person's free will. In his final observation, Tillotson argues that in spite of its necessary limitations, faith is a sufficient principle for life; he can assert this for two reasons. The first (oddly, given what has preceded it) is the 'sufficient assurance of the truth of these things'. Reason persuades us of this (as is implicit in our understanding of divine providence) while revelation confirms reason. The second is that it is important that we believe these things. For this, he falls back on a version of Pascal's wager: 'For as for the other world, if at the last there should prove to be no such thing, our condition after death will be the same with the condition of those who disbelieve these things; because all will be extinguished by death: but if things fall out otherwise (as most undoubtedly they will) and our souls after this life do pass into a state of everlasting happiness or misery, then our great interest plainly lies in preparing ourselves for this state.'[10] Tillotson can now apply what he has demonstrated; his inference is that Christians need a strong element of rationality in their faith in order that it might be strong enough to withstand any pressures. It is not unreasonable, he concludes, to meditate on our hopes of everlasting life 'to make it the great business of this present and temporal life, to secure a future and blessed happiness'.[11]

The logic is tight throughout the sermon. There is no place for anecdote; such examples as there are are used to make a

---

10 *op. cit.*, p. 195.
11 *op cit.*, p. 200.

reasonable point, as, for example, when Tillotson compares faith in eternal life to the attitude of businessmen who invest in the produce of countries they have never visited (and of whose existence, therefore, they can only know by report). The Wilkins model suited well the Latitudinarian mindset which emphasized simplicity and rationality, held that revelation confirmed the essential truths which were accessible to all people through reason, and that beyond those essential truths other religious opinions were *adiaphora*.[12]

This mindset was to be a dominant ecclesiastical force in eighteenth-century England. The Latitudinarian hold on the Church of England which began under William and Mary eased only a little in the last five years of Queen Anne and was strengthened by the long years of Whig government under the first two Georges. It was in this period that Britain (along with the American colonies and parts of central Europe) experienced an awakening in religion that was to transform the ecclesiastical landscape. The evangelical revival in Britain can be understood in part as a reaction against the Whig–Latitudinarian hegemony. It would be simplistic to see the early Methodists as picking up the baton of the non-jurors or to argue that the denial of preferment to those of High Church opinion freed the energy which was to drive the revival, but both of those factors played a part in the genesis of the movement of which George Whitefield and the Wesley brothers were to become leaders. The Society for the Promotion of Christian Knowledge also played a part, developing the network of corresponding members through whom the Pietism of Spener and Halle came to be known in the British Isles. For all that Pietism may have originated in opposition to Lutheran orthodoxy in Germany, its claims were equally opposed to the generalities of Latitudinarianism, demanding of its adherents a personal faith and a life-transforming commitment to works of piety and the fellowship of believers. A religion that appealed not to the mind but to the heart and which drew its authority not only from reason and revelation but also from the claims

---

12 K. Hylson-Smith, *The Churches in England from Elizabeth I to Elizabeth II*, vol. 2, London: SCM Press, 1997, p. 22.

of experience was far from the gentle, measured approach of Tillotson and those who came after him.

Preaching was, of course, central to the evangelical revival. It was through their preaching above all else that Daniel Rowland, Howell Harris, George Whitefield and John Wesley convinced thousands of their need for vital faith. Much of that preaching was offered in the open air, but the evangelicals were on occasions to occupy the pulpits of the established Church and, from the 1740s onwards, to have their own buildings provided through Wesley's galvanizing of his Methodist societies or the generosity and interest of Selina, Countess of Huntingdon, or other noble or gentle benefactors. The preaching was also circulated in print, although there are questions over whether what could be read as the preaching of Whitefield or Wesley was actually what was heard by the crowds who gathered in the fields to listen to them or the assemblies of Methodists in their preaching houses. Old cannot believe that Whitefield preached extemporaneously the closely argued treatises on matters of theology which appear in the *Selected Sermons*,[13] and Albert Outler has argued that some of Wesley's oral sermons never appeared in print and some of those in print were never preached orally.[14] It is not unlikely that there are elements of the live delivery which were not reproduced when the sermons were sent to the press; one looks in vain through the Whitefield corpus for the moments of dramatic tension that had noblemen shouting as if they were at a pantomime. The printed versions are all that the modern scholar has; they would have taken their place in the libraries of the day alongside those of other clergymen (and indeed of those who were not clergymen who nevertheless wrote sermons as part of their literary output).

The theology of Whitefield and Wesley could not be more different from that of the Latitudinarians, but their use of sermon form is not. It is simply not true that Whitefield's sermons 'lack structure'.[15] Many of them are organized on the Wilkins schema.

---

13 H. O. Old, *The Reading and Preaching of the Scriptures in the Worship of the Christian Church*, vol. 5: *Moderation, Pietism, and Awakening*, Grand Rapids: Wm Eerdmans, 2004, p. 149.

14 Edwards, *op. cit.*, vol. 1, p. 440.

15 Old, *op. cit.*, vol. 5, p. 153.

Whitefield may present more than three parts when he outlines what he is going to say, but they can be seen to fall within the plain pattern of explication, confirmation, and application. So, in one of his most famous sermons, 'The Lord our Righteousness',[16] Whitefield proposes

> through divine grace,
> I. To consider who we are to understand by the word Lord.
> II. How the Lord is man's righteousness.
> III. I will consider some of the chief objections that are generally urged against this doctrine.
> IV. I shall show some very ill consequences that flow naturally from denying this doctrine.
> V. Shall conclude with an exhortation to all to come to Christ by faith, that they may be enabled to say with the prophet in the text, 'The Lord our righteousness.'

The first and second of these divisions form the explication, the third the confirmation, and the last two the application. As Whitefield was preaching for conversion, it is not surprising to find that heavy emphasis is laid on the application, but even so, this is preaching as Wilkins would have recognized it – teaching clearly, convincing strongly and persuading powerfully.

The published sermons of John Wesley show a less consistent use of the Wilkins model. It is often stated that Wesley was a very different preacher from Whitefield, but the inference that Wesley was a quiet academic whilst Whitefield an extravagant thespian would be more than the evidence can bear. Wesley was known on occasions to preach with 'very vulgar enthusiasm',[17] but that is not (and cannot be) captured in the four volumes which remain to us. The published sermons may be no more than the skeletons of Wesley's addresses. He claimed never to have preached from notes after 1738,[18] although he seems to have kept a detailed

---

16 *Selected Sermons of George Whitefield* <http://www.ccel.org/ccel/whitefield/sermons.html> – accessed 28th August 2008.

17 John Chute in correspondence to Horace Walpole, quoted in G. Best, *Charles Wesley*, Peterborough: Epworth, 2006, p. 273.

18 H. Rack, *Reasonable Enthusiast*, London: Epworth, 1989, p. 345.

record of which sermons he preached in which places.[19] These
are identified only by their texts, so the relation of the register
to the published corpus of sermons cannot be discerned with
certainty. Eye-witness accounts of Wesley's preaching suggest far
more anecdotal and illustrative material (and far greater length)
than is apparent from the printed offerings.[20] These factors are
frustrating for the present study, but it was never Wesley's intention to leave to the historian evidence of his preaching. The sermons were published in order to clarify the doctrinal basis of the
Methodist revival, and to do so in an easily understood form:

> But I am throughly sensible, these [doctrines] are not proposed
> in such a manner as some may expect. Nothing here appears
> in an elaborate, elegant, or oratorical dress. If it had been my
> desire or design to write thus, my leisure would not permit.
> But, in truth, I, at present, designed nothing less; for I now
> write, as I generally speak, *ad populum*, to the bulk of man-
> kind, to those who neither relish nor understand the art of
> speaking; but who, notwithstanding, are competent judges of
> those truths which are necessary to present and future happi-
> ness. I mention this, that curious readers may spare themselves
> the labour of seeking for what they will not find.[21]

Assuming that the form of the published version in some way
approximates to that of a delivered sermon, Wesley was a fol-
lower of the plain style, though with a flexible approach to
his structure. Asked for guidance on 'What is the best general
method of preaching?' his response was:

(1.) To invite.
(2.) To convince.
(3.) To offer Christ.
(4.) To build up; and to do this in some measure in every
      sermon.[22]

19 N. Curnock (ed.), *The Journal of the Reverend John Wesley*, vol. 8, London: Epworth, 1938, pp. 171–252.

20 Rack, *op. cit.*, pp. 346f.

21 *Forty-Four Sermons*, London: Epworth, 1944, p. v.

22 John Wesley, *Works*, London: Wesleyan Conference Office, 1872, vol. 8,
p. 369.

The last two points reflect the tension apparent in preaching to two classes within the congregation. From a theology which emphasized not only personal salvation but the possibility of the assurance of personal salvation, the early Methodist was charged with attempting to bring those so far unregenerate to the point of conversion and encouraging those already converted on the path to perfection. But method (unless Wesley simply ignored his own advice) was not equivalent to form.

Wesley's own sermons are closely argued essays. His approach was invariably to take a text of Scripture and to ask of it (or of a doctrine which he discovers to be closely related to it) a number of questions. Almost every sermon can be reduced to 'what does this mean?' and the number of divisions will be either the number of ideas in the text that merit consideration or the number of angles from which the concept needs to be considered. In some respects, it is an approach similar to that taken by Wycliffe, although Wesley is more likely to alert the congregation to the direction he is taking. So, in his sermon on 'Justification by Faith',[23] Wesley sets out to show 'First. What is the general ground of this whole doctrine of justification. Secondly. What justification is. Thirdly. Who they are that are justified. And, fourthly. On what terms they are justified.'[24] Where the text is controversial, as in 'The great privilege of those who are born of God',[25] Wesley would stay close to the text defining each of its clauses. The same method is adopted even when the substance of the sermon is at a distance from the original meaning of the text, as in 'The Catholic Spirit'[26] where Wesley divides what he has to say about the possibilities and the necessity of Christians having fellowship across confessional boundaries according to the two parts of the conversation between Jehu and Jehonadab in 2 Kings 10.15. On other occasions, a controversial subject necessitated an approach from a number of standpoints; when it came to the subject of reason, Wesley wanted to reject both the

---

23 *Works* vol. 5, pp. 120–32.
24 *Works* vol. 5, p. 121.
25 *Works* vol. 5, pp. 305–16.
26 *Works* vol. 5, pp. 595–608.

irrationalism of some within the revival and the overdependence on rational thought of the Latitudinarians. This approach was shown when he preached on 'In understanding be men' (1 Cor. 14.20).[27] He tackled his subject from two angles, addressing himself first to those who overvalued and then to those who undervalued reason. The tightness of his argument is demonstrated by his refusal to proceed to the body of his material before he had defined the word 'reason' to his own satisfaction; the Wilkins model and the distinction between sermon and essay are apparent in the closing section which offers 'a few plain words' to those who have been prone to either mistake.

Sermon form for Wesley was not a matter of rule. It served his purpose, which was always to prove his point with as much clarity (and erudition) as possible. If it was from him or his contemporaries that the simple three-decker sermon so beloved of preachers in the following two centuries originated,[28] this was almost a coincidence. Famous examples of it such as 'The Use of Money'[29] ('Gain all you can. Save all you can. Give all you can.') and 'The Marks of the New Birth'[30] (which Wesley identifies as faith, hope and love) are results of Wesley's invariable approach; it just so happens that the appropriate answer to the question 'what does this mean?' is threefold in each instance, though Wesley would not have been ignorant of the mnemonic value of such a simple structure.

It was neither Wesley nor Whitefield who gave evangelical preaching a distinct and serviceable structure. That was the achievement of a man on whom apparently neither of the great preachers of the awakening had any direct effect. Charles Simeon was born in 1759. His religious development up until the age of 19 appears to have been unremarkable, but within a few weeks of his arrival at King's College, Cambridge, as an undergraduate, he was a changed man. His evangelical conversion was the result of a spiritual crisis provoked by a routine expectation that

---

27 'The Case of Reason impartially considered', *Works* vol. 6, pp. 389–400.
28 Rack, *op. cit.*, p. 345.
29 *Works* vol. 2, pp. 147–59.
30 *Works* vol. 5, pp. 293–304.

he would attend the communion service in the college chapel. Intense self-examination convinced him that he was no more fit to receive the Eucharist than Satan himself and, apparently without any guidance, he devoted himself to the search for a solution to his condition. During Holy Week 1779, he came to a realization of the value of the atoning sacrifice of Christ for his sins and celebrated Easter with joy.[31] He was for the remainder of his undergraduate days a lonely evangelical. It was only when he became a Fellow that he was drawn into the group of like-minded young men of whom the minister at St Edwards, Christopher Atkinson, was one. The *éminence grise* of the group was one of the leaders of the Anglican evangelicals, Henry Venn, who came to exercise a considerable influence over Simeon and drew him into the Clapham Sect.

The rest of Simeon's life was to be spent in Cambridge. He was ordained deacon in 1782 and, most unusually (apparently due to the influence of his father with the Bishop of Ely), was given the living of Holy Trinity in September of the same year.[32] The appointment was not welcome to the churchwardens, who insisted on appointing their own candidate as Lecturer and refusing Simeon the use of his own church whenever they could. In spite of the difficulties, the young Simeon quickly made an impression and began to draw larger congregations to his services. Continuing to live in King's (where he was also far from popular because of his 'serious' views), he developed a ministry to the university's students, particularly identifying evangelicals and encouraging them to offer for ordination. Because so many participated in his conversation parties and sermon classes as well as hearing him preach, Simeon was to exercise an enormous influence within the Church of England's clergy for half a century; H. E. Hopkins reckons that at least 600 of the students who sat at Simeon's feet went on to serve as priests.[33] Never a poor man, he used his wealth to further evangelical causes and

---

31 H. E. Hopkins, *Charles Simeon of Cambridge*, Grand Rapids: Wm Eerdmans, 1977, pp. 27ff.

32 Hopkins, *op. cit.*, pp. 36f.

33 *Charles Simeon, Preacher Extraordinary*, Bramcote: Grove Books, 1979, p. 33.

bought up livings in order that (despite the continued suspicion of 'Methodism' within the Church in the early nineteenth century) his protégés might not be without appointment. At a time when, as he lamented to the Archbishop of Canterbury in 1832,[34] programmes for the formation of the clergy were non-existent, Simeon saw it as his peculiar mission to enable some of those who (armed with a sufficient knowledge of Greek and a Cambridge degree) could expect to be ordained to have some understanding of the spiritual dimension of the vocation that was to be theirs.

His sense of calling to this mission stemmed from the complete lack of pre-ordination training that he himself had received. The demands made on those who would read for a Cambridge degree in the 1780s were not onerous[35] and the concept of a personal vocation (which forms part of the selection process in most denominations today) was wholly alien to a culture in which the Church was seen as an alternative gentry profession to the army for those without land. Dissenters had their own academies to train their ministers (who were excluded from admission to Oxford or Cambridge), but nothing approximating to an Anglican theological college for those accepted for the ministry existed nor was any such institution envisaged. (Selina, Countess of Huntingdon, had set up an establishment at Howell Harris' home in Wales to prepare lay preachers to seek ordination in the Church of England but the refusal of bishops to accept her candidates meant that this too became a Dissenters' college.) Having entered into his ministry with little preparation apart from the theology that he had taught himself and the encouragement of Henry Venn, Simeon was determined to do something to address this situation.

Part of the lack of training that he lamented was in preaching. He confessed that when he was ordained he 'did not know the head from the tail of a sermon'.[36] It was only in the 1790s that

---

34 *Horae Homileticae*, London: Holdsworth and Ball, 1832–33, vol. 1, pp. if.

35 Hopkins, *Charles Simeon of Cambridge*, p. 32.

36 Hopkins, *op. cit.*, p. 57.

he discovered the manual which was, through him, to be influential.[37] By that time, he had established in his own mind the principles on which his preaching was to be based. First, a sermon should always be doxological: 'For the whole course of his ministry Simeon worked at making Anglican preaching a significant means of serving God's glory.'[38] One of the features which distinguishes Simeon from Whitefield and Wesley is the liturgical underpinning of the Cambridge minister's work. Simeon was a devoted user of the Book of Common Prayer and saw preaching as an accompaniment to the faithful and reverent performance of the prescribed liturgy. Second, preaching was biblical. It was Henry Venn who encouraged Simeon to see the Bible as the primary source book for his sermons;[39] Simeon's stated aim in preaching was to make of his congregation 'Bible Christians'.[40] The Bible in his understanding was a compendium of doctrine through which humankind was blessed; the task of the preacher was to unfold what was compressed in the text,[41] and this ministry of unfolding also had to be understood biblically, as to Simeon the Bible was a self-interpreting revelation. What it revealed, above all, was Christ, so, third, Simeon's understanding of preaching was Christocentric. The minutes of the Eclectic Society, a group of evangelical Christians who met for discussion on a wide range of issues from 1783 onwards, record that 'all members agreed that Jesus Christ was the grand subject of the sermon'.[42] What Simeon aimed to do above all else in his preaching was to bring debased sinners face to face with the exalted Saviour in order that they might experience the merits of his passion.[43]

The manual which offered Simeon a clear structure for doing this was written by a seventeenth-century French Huguenot. Jean Claude's *Essay on the Composition of a Sermon* came into

---

37 Hopkins, *op. cit.*, p. 58.
38 Old, *op. cit.* vol. 5, pp. 566f.
39 Hopkins, *Preacher Extraordinary*, p. 7.
40 Hopkins, *op. cit*, p. 20.
41 Old, *op. cit.*, vol. 6, p. 570.
42 J. H. Pratt, *Eclectic Notes*, London, 2nd edn, 1865, p. 23.
43 *Horae Homileticae* vol. 1, pp. xixff.

Simeon's hands through the translation of the Cambridge Baptist minister, Robert Robinson. Simeon published it with some of his own sermon outlines in 1796 and appended a new translation of it, with annotations, to his final edition of the *Horae Homileticae*. The central virtue of preaching which Simeon drew from Claude was perspicuity. The aim of preaching was to make known the truth that the scriptural text contained and to do so clearly and purely. This was the first of Claude's six 'general rules'.[44] Simeon believed that three things were indispensable to effective preaching: unity in the design of the sermon, perspicuity in the arrangement and simplicity in the delivery.[45] The whole of his homiletic approach is expressed in those three ideas.

The working through of those three ideas spawned a prodigious output. Simeon's *magnum opus* was his *Horae Homileticae*. He began to publish what he called the 'skeletons' of his sermons in 1796.[46] This first collection of one hundred sermon outlines (with Claude's essay), grew to a five-volume publication within six years, to 17 volumes by 1819, and finally to 21 volumes in 1832. This definitive edition contained 2,536 'skeletons', arranged in the order of their text. He suggested that these might be used in devotional reading, and helpfully calculated that a pious person reading one a day would be sustained for exactly seven years.[47] But the target audience was the clergy. Simeon did not want to continue the practice of many eighteenth-century preachers of using someone else's material, but neither did he believe that all ministers should have to create their own sermons without help. His solution (which will seem to many to be far closer to the first practice than the latter) was to offer the outline of a sermon which the preacher could then make his own.[48] It is an approach very similar to that used by modern preachers' journals, which offer an abbreviated form of a sermon for each Sunday. The arrangement of the final compendium by biblical reference is illustrative of Simeon's hermeneutical principle. A

---

44 *Horae* vol. 21, p. 294.
45 *Horae* vol. 1, p. vi.
46 Hopkins, *Charles Simeon of Cambridge*, p. 59.
47 *Horae* vol. 1, p. xxviii.
48 *Horae* vol. 1, p. iv.

verse or passage of Scripture could have only one meaning and that was its historical and literal sense. Once the exegetical work had been done and the text interpreted by reference to other parts of the Bible it had given up all its secrets and there was no more to be said. For that reason, there could not be more than one sermon on any text, although Simeon did not disapprove of preaching the same sermon on more than one occasion.[49]

Claude argued from classical rhetoric that the five parts of an address can be reduced to three – the exordium, the discussion and the conclusion. The weight of the sermon is in the middle section, but the sermon needs an exordium in order to engage the congregation with the text. However, as the exordium is not the main business of the sermon it should be brief. Simeon recommended that six to twelve sentences sufficed. The object as Claude saw it was to get the congregation in a positive mood to listen. He therefore counselled that it be 'cool and grave' though Simeon noted that there might be exceptions to this rule.[50] Accounts of his own preaching report that his opening words were sometimes anything but 'cool and grave'. On one occasion, he followed his text from the book of Malachi, 'Will a man rob God?', by vehemently accusing the congregation of each having robbed him, pointing his finger at various members of the discomforted assembly.[51] By contrast, Simeon's advice to preachers in the last volume of the *Horae Homileticae* contains no recommendation to such violent language. He follows Claude's assertion that the exordium should be 'engaging and agreeable'.[52] On its relation to the biblical text, there is a touch of ambivalence. It needs to be connected to the text but it may not be unique to the sermon. Claude disapproved of common exordiums, but Simeon believed that an exordium that had worked as the opening to one sermon might with profit be reused to begin another. That was possible because the exordium should be general in tone. If following the Claude-Simeon model, a preacher should

---

49 *Horae* vol. 1, p. xxvi.
50 *Horae* vol. 21, p. 402.
51 Hopkins, *Charles Simeon of Cambridge*, p. 63.
52 *Horae* vol. 21, p. 403.

not start with a local, personal or ephemeral reference; Simeon would never have begun a sermon by talking about something that had occurred in the previous week or had happened on the way to the church.

The main body of the sermon was designed to do three things, according to Claude. There was the connexion, which related the text to that which had preceded it. Simeon held this to be important as a text should only be understood within its own context.[53] Then the text should be reduced to a single categorical proposition. For Simeon this was the key to the whole method; he made far more of this than Claude did.[54] That proposition then had to be discussed. By this method, Simeon believed, he could achieve both fidelity to the biblical message and freedom for the preacher. It would usually be necessary to divide the material into sections in order to discuss it and these should usually be laid out before the congregation. Claude argued that there should be no more than four or five divisions, and at best two or three. The divisions might emerge naturally from the text or they might need to be imposed by the reasoning of the argument that had been deduced from the text. From the division, the discussion would most often proceed in one of two ways – either by observation or by explication. The latter was more suitable if the text or subject were doctrinal, whereas observation was appropriate to a historical text. Sometimes, however, a text might demand both forms of treatment and sometimes neither. Clarity is always the aim; if the message of a text was already obvious, nothing was to be gained by either explication or observation, but the sermon could be one of continued application. Simeon was adept in moving from observation or explication to application almost imperceptibly.

Once the discussion has been completed, the preacher should move to a conclusion (which is also variously described as the peroration, address or application). Unlike the exordium, this part of the sermon should be lively and animated and should

---

53 *Horae* vol. 21, p. 341.
54 *Horae* vol. 21, p. 307.

aim to touch the emotions. The preacher has to recognize that the congregation listening is a mixed company and should offer reflections which are appropriate to different conditions and which reach people through different emotions. Four or five closing thoughts ought to suffice, and they should be arranged so that the last is the most powerful. Simeon would show in his skeletons how those who were at different stages of faith development were to be approached in this part of the sermon, so in his model sketch of a sermon on the longer ending of Mark's Gospel he asks questions first of unbelievers, then of those weak in faith and finally of committed and faithful Christians.

With 2536 skeletons from which to choose, it is impossible to offer a single example as 'typical' of Simeon's method and to do justice to his contribution to homiletics. But sermon 1064 can serve as illustrative of the structure that he derived from Claude. Entitled 'God will be found of sincere worshippers', this is a sermon on Jeremiah 29.11–14. Simeon begins with the simple observation that Jeremiah was writing at and about a time of calamity, but had discerned that the misfortunes of the Judaeans were part of God's (good) purposes. From this brief introduction he moves to the two parts of his discussion. Here Simeon's method is to observe the subject from two angles. From God's perspective, it is clear that his purpose of love and peace will be accomplished. About that there are three things to be said: that God wants peace, that it will happen in his time and that he will not disappoint those who base their expectations on the biblical promises. From the human perspective, these verses read as a call to fervent prayer, and a similar threefold development is offered. Prayer has been appointed by God, our circumstances should increase our desire to pray and those who pray faithfully will obtain God's blessing. A typical Simeon conclusion states that all this is of use to humble those who are proud, to awaken those who think that they are already secure in God's blessing, and to comfort those who are feeble-minded and anxious.

For more than 50 years, people came to hear Simeon preach at Holy Trinity and undergraduates learned from him both formally and informally the art of preaching. By the time of his death the

early hostility had long been forgotten and he was a remarkably popular figure in Cambridge;[55] his influence on the future
of Anglicanism, both in England and overseas, was already great
and increasing. How influential his teaching on preaching was is
more difficult to evaluate. What J. M. Neale called 'Mr Simeon's
one and twenty tedious volumes'[56] sold in huge numbers,[57] but
it is impossible to gauge whether or not the incumbents of the
parishes controlled by his or another evangelical trust were
adding their own flesh to Simeon's skeletons. More generally,
Simeon's advice represents a tradition that has continued for 200
years. Preaching, he often repeated, has three aims: 'to humble
the sinner, to exalt the Saviour, and to promote holiness'.[58] Those
who have heard mainstream evangelical preaching in the early
twenty-first century will see that his principles are still being
followed.

Whether his exegetical approach is still being followed is
another question. Simeon's method of preaching was predicated
on his understanding of Scripture. He was, as most of his contemporaries would have been, a literalist, and lived before the
period when the later nineteenth-century combination of biblical
criticism and Darwin's theory of evolution would persuade many
that such literalism was untenable. The twenty-first-century
preacher might want to argue that a different approach is needed
altogether and that the 21 volumes of skeletons are now no more
than museum pieces. For example, Simeon's sermon on Genesis
20.9, 'Abraham reproved for denying his wife', begins with a
statement of his admiration for 'the fidelity of Scriptural history'
which is prepared to relate events even if they cast a bad light
on otherwise heroic characters.[59] He then goes on in the main
part of the sermon to comment on Abraham's offence and on the
rebuke that he received. The closing exhortation suggests practical actions based on the moral lessons of the passage.

---

55 Hopkins, *Charles Simeon of Cambridge*, p. 205.
56 *Mediaeval Preachers and Mediaeval Preaching*, London, 1856, p. lxvi.
57 Edwards, *op. cit.*, vol. 1, p. 455.
58 *Horae* vol. 1, p. xxi.
59 *Horae* vol. 1, p. 145.

A modern reader might recoil at Simeon's opening gambit. This is a story that stretches the credibility of the reader who wants to understand it as 'faithful scriptural history'. According to Genesis 20, Abraham was living as a foreigner in the land of Gerar. Because he had claimed that Sarah was his sister and not his wife, the king, Abimelech, had taken Sarah into his harem. Abimelech was warned in a dream that the act (which he had not yet committed) was adulterous, and so he returned Sarah to Abraham. As Simeon notes, this was not the first time that Abraham reportedly tried to pass off his wife as his sister with unhappy results, and the reader is surprised that he had not learned his lesson. More remarkably, this second occasion comes after the writer has disclosed that Sarah is over 90 and well past the age of child-bearing (Gen. 17.17), so the reader wonders at Abimelech's interest in her. The story is riddled with inconsistencies. Abimelech first rebukes Abraham and then showers him with gifts, after which Abraham prays successfully for Abimelech to be healed, although we have not been told that he is ill. Modern (or even late nineteenth-century) biblical scholarship might conclude that the editors of Genesis have been conflating two or more traditions in this narrative.

There are other reasons for hesitation in approaching this story. Abraham apparently is Sarah's brother, or at least her half-brother. This incestuous relationship stands in clear violation of most social conventions (and of later Mosaic Law) and rings a particularly strange note after the incestuous behaviour of Lot's daughters related in the previous chapter. Also of concern to many modern readers of the text is the treatment of Sarah; it will seem repugnant to most if not all in a twenty-first-century western congregation that women should be treated as items of property in this manner. That those on whom a fraud has been perpetrated (Abimelech and his harem) are apparently dependent on the prayers of the fraudster (Abraham) for their future well-being is a detail which also raises serious questions about election. Abraham is the representative of God's chosen people, a status which still seems to give him enormous power however badly he behaves.

All these issues are part of the hermeneutics of suspicion. Unlike Simeon's auditory, a twenty-first century congregation cannot be asked simply to trust the text. Given that Simeon's entire work depended on approaching the text in precisely that way, does that mean that it is worthless to modern preachers? It is at this point that the approach of Paul Ricoeur can be of value; just as it was a French Protestant of the seventeenth century who gave Simeon a structure for his sermons, so a French Protestant of the twentieth century might be able to assist modern preachers to rediscover the utility of Simeon's skeletons.

Ricoeur developed 'the hermeneutics of suspicion and retrieval'. Complicated though his thought is, the approach can be briefly described as a way of accepting both the problems of the text and its value. Ricoeur argues that suspicions cannot be ignored. The author of a text had preconceptions which the reader may not share and had motives for writing which the reader may feel undercut the value of the text. The reader of the text comes with preconceptions which shape their interpretation of reality. But, argues Ricoeur, if we can recognize that the text is 'suspicious' and distance ourselves from it, then we can read it with 'a second naïveté'. There is a strange childlikeness about Ricoeur's suggested approach. We are called to play in the world in front of the text; 'in play subjectivity forgets itself'.[60] What the Bible reveals in this way is a new way of being; we come as people of hope (a vital concept for Ricoeur) to find new possibilities for our lives.

One of the distinctive parts of Simeon's approach to sermons was his attitude to the exordium, which he viewed as a semi-detached part of the structure.[61] The purpose of the exordium was to prepare the congregation to receive the message of the text; its relation to the text itself could be tangential. The modern preacher has a way into his skeletons, even into re-using them. So, taking the story of Abraham, Sarah, and Abimelech, the preacher might begin with a general introduction about the problems of

---

60 P. Ricouer (ed. & tr. J. B. Thompson), *Hermeneutics and the Human Sciences*, Cambridge: Cambridge University Press, 1981, p. 186.

61 See above, p. 116.

reading a text such as this. Rather than Simeon's praise for the fidelity of historical narrative the preacher expresses repugnance at the events described. Yet even while we are appalled, the argument might run, we can see some things that are common to human nature.

Simeon's two main sections can then be allowed to stand. The preacher might still want to focus first on Abraham's sin, naming it for what it is, and noting with Simeon that it originated in a lack of faith, in a natural concern for self-preservation, and in an all too human tendency to repeat even those sins of which we are ashamed. The preacher might then move on to analyse the rebuke that Abraham receives, noting that Abraham had to acknowledge his failure in charity, his failure in his duty as a husband, and the way that his sin affected others (Abimelech). With that, the preacher will contrast (as Simeon does) the moderation, equity and virtuousness shown by Abimelech. From this point the preacher can appropriately move into a series of exhortations, possibly repeating some of the four suggested by Simeon: that Christians should shun all forms of deception, avoid relapsing into previously committed sins, be thankful for the protection of God and work (as Abraham did) to undo the effects of their sins.

Simeon was aware that not everyone shared his theological preconceptions. On the great issue that split evangelicals in the eighteenth century (Arminianism *versus* Calvinism) he claimed to hold a moderating position and his desire was to be of service to the whole Church, not only to evangelicals. So that his skeletons might be useful to as broad a constituency as possible, they were laid out in different fonts, suggesting that some preachers might use only the main points and supplement them with their own material, while others might draw on some or all of his more detailed ideas. Two hundred years later, *mutatis mutandis*, the advice might still be appropriate.

6

'HEART SPEAKING TO HEART'

John Henry Newman

J. M. Neale's scathing dismissal of Simeon's *magnum opus*[1] was penned only 20 years after the death of the great Cambridge preacher, but it is indicative of a far wider change of approach. Neale and Simeon represent different schools within the Church of England but the difference between them can also be understood in terms of the culture of the day. Simeon had been the last great practitioner in England of preaching as part of the classical (or neo-classical) tradition; Claude's essay (like that of Wilkins) was a statement of classical principles. The difference between an Andrewes and a Tillotson sermon is the difference between the baroque and the classical, as much as is the difference between concerti by Vivaldi and Haydn, paintings by Rubens and Reynolds, or houses by Vanburgh and Nash. The range of names and the varied times at which their work occurs indicates that there can be no clear divisions between the periods, but in broad terms the seventeenth and eighteenth centuries saw a movement from the elaboration of the baroque to the clear lines of the classical in all forms of art. Where the baroque had favoured ornamentation, the classical favoured clarity; where the

---

1 Above, p. 119.

baroque had longed for a riot of colour and the complexity of polyphony, the classical had favoured clean lines and harmonic simplicity. Unsurprisingly, preaching reflected that broad cultural change. Where Andrewes had believed that elegance was achieved by wit, Tillotson maintained that it came from clear reasoning.

By the mid-nineteenth century broad cultural change had occurred again. A Schumann symphony differs from one by Mozart as does a poem by Shelley from one by Pope. The outward form may appear to be the same, but the content is vastly different. Where the classical movement had been typified by reason, objectivity and order, the romantic movement celebrated emotion, subjectivity and spontaneity. Where the classical artists had drawn their inspiration from ancient Greece and Rome, Romantics rediscovered the Gothic characteristics of the Middle Ages. The Romantics celebrated the human personality, exalting the genius and giving high status to the feelings and the natural world, exulting in untamed wildness. Whether it was in the visual arts, music or literature, what mattered was no longer the balance and elegance of the phrasing but the passion of the statement. There was a violence about the early Romantics, captured in the very notion of *Sturm und Drang*. Most significantly of all, the difference between the classical artist and the Romantic was the degree of involvement in the work. There is always a level of detachment in the classical approach; but the Romantics poured themselves into their art. Mozart produced great music in spite of his poverty and struggles; Schumann produced great music out of his disappointments and distress.

This cultural development had its effect in theology. The epitome of the movement in the history of Christian thought is represented by Friedrich Schleiermacher, arguably the most important western theologian after the Reformers. Schleiermacher (1768–1834) was at one with the *zeitgeist* of the Germany of his day. Known to the leading lights of cultural life in Berlin (such as the poet-philosopher Schlegel and the poet and dramatist Goethe), his book *On Religion: Speeches to its Cultured Despisers* made him 'the new darling of the Romantic movement'.[2] His achievement was to create a new way of think-ing about Christian faith, which he did by locating religion not in the area of knowledge nor of action but of feeling. 'Feeling' in Schleiermacher's vocabulary is not the weak word that it might seem to be, as if a human being's connection with ultimate real-ity were only about emotion and sensation. 'Feeling' refers to an intuition which seems to exist (according to Schleiermacher) in the pre-consciousness of the individual, an intuition of which religion is the highest expression.

> This is the peculiar sphere which I would assign to religion – the whole of it, and nothing more. Unless you grant it, you must either prefer the old confusion to clear analysis, or pro-duce something else, I know not what, new and quite wonder-ful. Your feeling is piety, in so far as it expresses, in the manner described, the being and life common to you and to the All. Your feeling is piety in so far as it is the result of the opera-tion of God in you by means of the operation of the world upon you. This series is not made up either of perceptions or of objects of perception, either of works or operations or of different spheres of operation, but purely of sensations and the influence of all that lives and moves around, which accompan-ies them and conditions them. These feelings are exclusively the elements of religion, and none is excluded.[3]

Schleiermacher's writings may not have been immediately influ-ential in England but Romanticism had its moment here and that affected the life of the Church. Just as Schleiermacher moved away from his Pietistic roots, so the man who can be cred-ited more than any other with changing the shape of preach-ing (and arguably of the Church in, not simply of, England) in the nineteenth century first stepped into a pulpit still a child of the Wesleyan revival. Like the German, he was also a product of the Romantic movement, who 'might have been thought of

2 Jonathan Hill, *History of Christian Thought*, Oxford: Lion, 2003, p. 224.

3 J. Oman (tr.), *On Religion: Speeches to its cultured despisers*, New York: Harper, 1965, pp. 46f.

as England's answer to Schleiermacher'.[4] John Henry Newman (1801–90) offers a unique insight into the ministry of preaching. At the end of his long life, he left homiletic material from both his Anglican and Roman Catholic days, material which displays different approaches but an essential unity of purpose. He also straddled another common division in preaching practice, that of university and parish, being at home in both the academic and the parochial environment and writing about the distinctive ministry of the university preacher.

In some respects, Newman's career mirrored Simeon's. It was, apparently, a matter of chance whether the young Newman was sent by his father to Oxford or to Cambridge;[5] the history of the Church of England could have been altogether different had the 16-year-old evangelical gone to sit at Simeon's feet, but the coach from London took him west rather than east. At Trinity College, Oxford, Newman appears to have been as isolated by his piety as Simeon had been at King's, Cambridge. Like Simeon, Newman having taken his degree looked set to remain for the rest of his life in the university town. Like Simeon, he was only a young man when he was invited to accept the living of his first (and only) parish, a leading pulpit with a congregation that included both town and gown. But there the paths diverge. Simeon proclaimed his unchanging truth from the same college, the same pulpit and the same Church, throughout his ministry. Newman studied the development of doctrine at Trinity and at Oriel, as both an Anglican and a Roman Catholic, in Oxford and elsewhere.

Like Simeon, Newman was something of a solitary individual but he was never alone in his activities. His progression from evangelical to High Churchman was gradual; it was after he had been in Oxford for six years that he became a fellow of Oriel College and met John Keble and Edward Pusey and later Hurrell Froude. These were like minds, concerned about the integrity

---

4 Hill, *op.cit.*, p. 249. Hill adds, 'had any Anglicans heard of the German theologian', which is a curious comment, as Newman certainly knew of Schleiermacher's work and viewed it with great suspicion and Pusey had studied in Berlin in the mid-1820s.

5 B. Martin, *John Henry Newman: His Life and Work*, London: Geoffrey Chapman Mowbray, 1990, p. 17.

of the Church which they perceived to be under threat from the indifference of its members and the interference of Parliament. Newman may have been seen as the leader of the Oxford movement for a period, but Keble was the older man and it was his assize sermon 'On the National Apostasy' that is commonly identified as the beginning of the movement. Because the movement is popularly associated with the development of liturgical practice (and its importance in that regard should never be underestimated), it is easy to forget that Pusey, Froude, Keble, Newman and the rest did not set out to recover the wearing of copes or the reservation of the blessed sacrament but the animation of religion.[6] Their aim was to recall a nominally Christian nation to the serious practice of its faith and a national Church to an appreciation of its own catholicity. Six months after the Keble sermon, the first of the tracts (by Newman) appeared, to be followed, over an eight-year period, by a series of (mainly anonymous) publications which were widely circulated. These laid out the main themes of the Tractarians but the greatest controversy followed the last (Tract 90) in which Newman argued that assent to the Thirty-nine Articles did not preclude a Catholic interpretation of them. Newman was aiming to persuade some of his associates (and himself) that their vocation was still to remain within the Church of England. The outcry that it provoked helped to convince him otherwise.

The publication of Tract 90 can be seen as a Rubicon for Newman but the story of his decision to leave the Church in which he had been baptized was a difficult and tortuous one. Tract 90 had been part of a series (of which Tracts 38 and 41 were the beginning) intended to demonstrate that Anglicanism is not a Protestant sect but a *via media* between the position of the Reformed and Roman Catholic Churches. The Church of England as it was, the Tractarians contended, was not the Church of England of its own reformers, and not the Church of what they regarded as the golden age of Andrewes and Laud. But the

---

6 Horton Davies, *Worship & Theology in England*, vol. 3, *From Watts and Wesley to Maurice*, Princeton: Princeton University Press, 1995, p. 244; L. Bouyer, 'Great Preachers 13: John Henry Newman', *Theology* 55 (1952), p. 88.

more Newman read church history, the more his own patristic studies persuaded him that this position was untenable; comparison with the Donatists or the Monophysites proved to him that 'The Church of Rome will be found right after all.'[7] There could be no *via media* between truth and error. 'I had nothing more to learn.'[8] 'The parting of friends',[9] painful though it was, was now inevitable, although Newman did not go alone. Several of the young men who lived in the community that he had established at Littlemore chose to share his journey into the Church of Rome.

By the time Newman made his final decision to become a Roman Catholic, he had already resigned the living of St Mary's, Oxford. It had been there that his reputation as a preacher was first established. He consciously rejected the approach of Simeon.[10] It was rarely his practice to divide his text or subject and if he appealed to the emotions of his congregation it was through the power and content of his thought rather than through any deliberate use of eloquence. Newman distrusted oratorical devices.[11] The accounts of his preaching (though often from fervent admirers, such as Froude) have him reading a carefully prepared script in a way that focused the congregation's attention not on the preacher but on the sermon. He had a studied method of not obtruding into his message; according to Owen Chadwick, Newman 'disappeared into the reality of which he spoke'.[12] But there can be little doubt that it was the man as much as, if not more than, the message which drew large numbers to St Mary's on a Sunday evening. For all that he loathed the idea of a personality cult, Newman always attracted admirers. Ellison may have overstated the situation when he spoke of Newman as a 'virtually super-

---

7 J. H. Newman (ed. I. Ker), *Apologia pro Vita Sua*, London: Penguin, 1994, p. 116.

8 *Apologia*, p. 183.

9 The title of Newman's last sermon as an Anglican.

10 E. Mackerness, *Heeded Voice: Studies in the Literary Status of the Anglican sermon*, Cambridge: W. Heffer, 1959, p. 4.

11 E. Griffiths, 'Newman: The Foolishness of Preaching', in I. Ker and A. Hill (eds), *Newman after a Hundred Years*, Oxford: Clarendon Press, 1990, p. 68.

12 O. Chadwick, *Newman*, Oxford: Oxford University Press, 1983, p. 21.

natural presence in nineteenth-century Oxford',[13] but Newman's evident asceticism contributed to the impression that the congregation was listening to a man 'who so evidently lived in a world far from their own'.[14] That there is a cause for his canonization proceeding at Rome at present would not have surprised many of his contemporaries, although it would have surprised the man himself. 'Saints are not literary men,' he maintained;[15] part of the reason for the respect in which Newman was regarded as a preacher was his ability to use the English language with eloquence and lucidity. There was a simple beauty about his prose. Among the admirers was a future Prime Minister:

> There was not very much change in the inflection of the voice; action there was none. His sermons were read, and his eyes were always bent on his book, and all that, you will say, is against efficiency in preaching. Yes, but you must take the man as a whole, and there was a stamp and a seal upon him; there was a solemn sweetness and music in the tone, there was a completeness in the figure, taken together with the tone and the manner, which made even his delivery, such as I have described it, and though exclusively from written sermons, singularly attractive.[16]

Not all those who have studied Newman's preaching agree. Charles Smyth was particularly scathing, although his contention that it was 'extraordinarily difficult to regard Newman in any other light than as an Evangelical gone to the bad' alerts the reader that this is not the most impartial of assessments.[17] Smyth found it difficult to understand why Newman's sermons were so 'exaggeratedly praised'[18] and maintained that the congregations

---

13 R. H. Ellison, *The Victorian Pulpit: Spoken and Written Sermons in Nineteenth-century Britain*, London: Associated University Presses, 1998, p. 88.

14 E. T. Vaughan, 'J. H. Newman as a Preacher', *Contemporary Review* 10 (1869), p. 40.

15 Martin, *op. cit.*, p. 156.

16 W. E. Gladstone, quoted in D. O'Connell (ed.), *Favorite Newman Sermons*, Milwaukee: Bruce, 1932 (reprinted: Kessinger, 1997), p. 3.

17 C. Smyth, *The Art of Preaching: A Practical Survey of Preaching in the Church of England 747–1939*, London, 1940, p. 222.

18 Smyth, *op. cit.*, p. 224.

at St Mary's and elsewhere must have been subjected to the reading of uninspired essays. Newman, according to Smyth, had no
natural affinity with spoken English, though his assertion that
the author of *The Dream of Gerontius* had no ear for poetry is
the most extraordinary part of his extraordinary critique. This
may (again) reflect the differing temper of different times. Newman was 'a child of the Romantic Revival',[19] though he was
never as fully a part of a Romantic movement as Schleiermacher
had been. The Oxford movement (largely through the influence
of Froude) was influential in the revival of interest in mediaeval practice and Newman as a preacher had the ability to speak
to the senses and the emotions. Cold reason was distrusted by
the Tractarians, but so was too much emotionalism, and they
had little time for the liberalism, libertarianism and libertinism
which marked many of the artistic Romantics. Yet Newman
understood the Romantic imagination (his two novels stand as
evidence of that) and he was infected by it. Where the rational-
ists trusted modern reason and the individual mind, Newman
based his case on the appeal to the past and the continuous line
of tradition. Reason had its limits and it left no room for the awe
which was essential to the Romantic mind; Newman was not
afraid of mystery and saw it as a crucial element of faith. '[This]
is the mysterious state in which Christians stand . . . they are in
Heaven, in the world of spirits, and are placed in the way of all
manner of invisible influences.'[20] What kept this from being mere
fantasy for Newman was its secure anchorage in the tradition of
the Church. Standing firmly in a tradition that embraced all that
had preceded the Reformation, even the Anglican Newman was
prepared to call himself 'an English Catholic'. With his sense
of mystery and dependence on history, Edwards can conclude
fairly that 'Newman was without doubt one of the great English
Romantic preachers'.[21]

---

19 Lytton Stracey, *Eminent Victorians* quoted in Martin, p. 9.

20 *Parochial and Plain Sermons*, London, 1844, vol. 3, p. 290.

21 O. C. Edwards, *A History of Preaching*, vol. 1, Nashville: Abingdon Press,
2004, p. 608. There is a considerable debate on the extent to which it is appropriate to refer to Newman as a Romantic. See Edwards, *op. cit.*, vol. 1, p. 621
for details of the bibliography.

Victorian readers agreed. Newman began to publish his Oxford sermons during his ministry at St Mary's, but agreed to a new edition as late as 1868. *Parochial and Plain Sermons* in eight volumes sold in large numbers throughout the Victorian period. That there is no corresponding collection of his preaching as a Roman Catholic is the result of a decision that he took during his seminary training. Roman priests, he was told, did not read their sermons, so Newman did not read his thereafter.[22] He distrusted the extempore, however, so his sermons were delivered from his recollection of carefully prepared notes. Some of those notes were published posthumously by the brothers of the Birmingham Oratory as *The Sermon Notes of John Henry Newman*. In a few cases, sermons were either prepared in full or written up from notes after delivery and then published, as *Discourses to Mixed Congregations* in 1849 and *Sermons Preached on Various Occasions* in 1874.

In addition to sermons, Newman left a little of his thinking about the preaching ministry, though he repeatedly claimed that it was not a subject on which he felt qualified to teach others. In the same year as the *Parochial and Plain Sermons* were reissued, Newman received a letter from a student at Maynooth, asking for advice on the preparation of sermons. Newman replied that he was diffident about offering any counsel on this subject.[23] Each preacher had to form his own style and should aim not at eloquence but at accuracy, power, comprehensibility and brevity. If the preacher could say 'simply and exactly what he feels or thinks, what religion demands, what faith teachers, [and] what the Gospel promises' eloquence would follow.[24] To that end Newman could only advise that the preacher needed to be humble and earnest. This last point was developed in a longer discussion about preaching in *The Idea of a University*. Newman's involvement with the establishment of the Catholic University in Dublin from 1853 onwards was not a period that he found at all happy,

22 I. Ker, *The Genius of John Henry Newman*, Oxford: Clarendon Press, 1992, p. 122.

23 Dessain, C. J., et al. (eds), *The Letters and Diaries of John Henry Newman*, Oxford: Clarendon Press, 1978, vol. XXIV, pp. 44f.

24 *Letters and Diaries* vol. XXIV, pp. 44f.

partly because of his own refusal to devote himself wholeheart-
edly to the task. But it did cause him to produce a series of nine
lectures in which he outlined what he believed the purpose of the
new institution to be. To these were added a number of other
lectures later in the 1850s, one of which was on 'University
Preaching'. In this he developed the idea that there were some
aspects about preaching in a university which demanded a distinct approach, though there were some things that could and
should be said about all sermons. Chief among these was the
purpose towards which the act of preaching should be directed.
The preacher's aim was to achieve some definite spiritual benefit
in the life of his hearers.[25] It was in this context that Newman's
stress on earnestness had to be understood. Preachers should not
try to be earnest; they should study their subject, the hope of
eternal life and the promise of judgement, so that they might
communicate something of that to those who needed to hear of
it. That would make them earnest.

In some ways, the thinking about the practice of preaching in
The Idea of a University marked a rejection of Newman's own
method in Oxford. There he had quite openly read his sermons;
to his Dublin audience he asserted that 'preaching is not reading
and reading is not preaching'.[26] However, it might, he believed,
be necessary to produce a manuscript in advance of the preaching. Newman's method of thinking things through was usually
with pen and paper; he even prayed that way.[27] Such thorough
preparation was essential, whether the manuscript was to be
hidden in the pulpit, reduced to notes, or simply left behind in
the study. Newman also asserts the importance of the preacher's
personality (which he had appeared to deny in Oxford). Preaching was not like celebrating the sacraments. A priest saying mass
is the same as any other priest but a priest's personality cannot
be invisible when preaching. 'Nothing that is anonymous will
preach.'[28] The preacher had to have a definite subject; he had

---

25 *The Idea of a University Defined and Illustrated*, London, 1907, p. 408.
26 *Idea*, p. 424.
27 Chadwick, *op. cit.*, p. 11.
28 *Idea*, p. 426.

to have a definite audience in mind; he had to be a definite individual. It would be wrong, however, to stress too strongly that this is a disparaging of his earlier Anglican practice. As has been shown, if Newman attempted to hide in his preaching before 1845, he failed; the difference may simply be that the Roman Catholic Newman was far more secure in his vocation, both as a theologian and as a pastor, than he had been in his Anglican period.

In other ways there is continuity between the preaching of the two parts of Newman's career. One of those is in the ability that Newman had to identify the needs of his auditory. Here he followed Aristotle's belief that the 'very essence of the Art [of Rhetoric lies] in the precise recognition of a hearer'.[29] The Christian preacher

> is, when in the pulpit, instructing, enlightening, informing, advancing, sanctifying, not all nations, nor all classes, nor all callings, but those particular ranks, professions, states, ages, characters, which have gathered around him. Proof indeed is the same all over the earth; but he has not only to prove, but to persuade; – *Whom?* A hearer, then, is included in the very idea of preaching; and we cannot determine how in detail we ought to preach, till we know whom we are to address.[30]

Like Schleiermacher, Newman had an understanding of his ministry and of theology that was essentially incarnational. The gospel came alive in particular instances; a sermon was this particular message from this particular preacher for these particular hearers. It was this understanding that made Newman the effective preacher he was in Oxford. He could lay 'his finger gently on a believer's heart and tell him things about himself that he had not known until then'[31] and appeared to speak individually to each member of his congregation.[32]

---

29 *Idea*, p. 416.

30 *Idea*, p. 416.

31 J. Tolhurst (quoting Professor Shairp), *Sermon Notes 1849–78 (edited by the Fathers of the Birmingham Oratory)*, Louisville: University of Notre Dame Press, 2000, p. xx.

32 Ellison, *op. cit.*, p. 84.

Central to Newman's approach was his belief that a sermon should never have more than one idea. He wrote to the Maynooth seminarian 'the great thing seems to be to have your subject distinctly before you . . . to take care that it should be one subject, not several'.[33] He argued at Dublin that to have more than one subject, even though that had been the practice of many great preachers, could only lead either (if they were preached together) to confusion as one subject would distract both preacher and listener from understanding another or (if they were preached in succession) to a series of sermons masquerading as a single address.[34] Newman was relentless in this singularity of aim. 'Sacrifice every thought, however good or clever, which does not tend to bring out your one point,' he advised the novice preacher at Maynooth. It was advice that could have come from the Oxford days and is displayed in the *Parochial and Plain Sermons*. Even Smyth grudgingly conceded that 'the only point on which it is possible to learn from John Henry Newman is the internal unity of his sermons'.[35] From this tight structure came the brevity which was always a feature; unusually for the time, Newman's Oxford sermons were of no more than a quarter of an hour's duration.[36]

Distinguished by this tight approach to subject matter, Newman's sermons do not have (as do Simeon's) a distinct structure. But, careful literary compositions that they are, they are never formless. 'Forms are the food of faith.'[37] Simeon may have seen his preaching as being like a telescope bringing the subject into clearer view with each division,[38] but Newman's method is far more illustrative of that idea. Newman preached in order to force a decision; his sermons were based on an intimate knowledge of the doctrine of the Church but they present that doctrine in such a way that it demands not only to be believed but to be

---

33 *Letters and Diaries* vol. XXIV, p. 44.
34 *Idea*, p. 412.
35 *The Art of Preaching*, p. 225.
36 Bouyer, *op. cit.*, p. 87.
37 Newman, quoted by Chadwick in I. Ker (ed.), *Selected Sermons*, New York: Paulist Press, 1994, p. 5.
38 Smyth, *op. cit.*, p. 176.

the basis for Christian action.[39] The Oxford sermons depended
heavily on Scripture in a way that the Roman Catholic ones do
not, but in both cases doctrine is brought to bear in such a way
that the listeners know they are being asked to respond.

A typical example of this is his sermon from the Catholic period
on the Feast of Mary Magdalene.[40] This is particularly interesting because it has an appendix which suggests that it could be
used in another way (though the very brief notes make it difficult
to reconstruct what Newman proposed might have been a better
homily). As with many of Newman's later sermons, the particular 'target audience' (in the fuller version) are potential converts
from Protestantism (of whom there seem to have been a number attending worship at the Birmingham Oratory). The sermon
begins with the Gospel story of Mary anointing the feet of Jesus
which he notes that she does irrespective of the opinion of others
at the meal table. He points out how remarkable this is, given
that it appears to be a common condition to need to consider
'what people will think of us'. At its worst, the feeling leads to
the tyranny of fashion, but Newman does not assault his hearers.
The concern is natural; therefore it is from God; therefore it is
not bad in itself. In fact, it could be good; those who have no
true religion are often guided by their concern for the favourable
opinion of others into doing good things. What Newman has
done here is to manoeuvre his listeners to a place where they can
accept his next point. Because they are not irreligious people,
they can see the error that others have made – to put fashion in
place of God, which is a bad thing.

Having, as it were, secured that agreement, Newman returns
to the Gospel story. He moves from Mary's action through a
number of scenarios in which it was probable that a person's
actions would meet with disapproval, from the minor point of
being careful as to which clothes are worn to church to 'being
ashamed to be known to pray'. Having recognized the failings
into which many of the congregation are likely to have fallen,
Newman offers a number of positive examples from the lives of

39 Bouyer, *op. cit.*, p. 88.
40 *Sermon Notes*, ed. Tolhurst, pp. 5–6.

the saints. He is not urging eccentric behaviour, but only that his hearers act seeking to please God not other people. Finally, he concludes with his word to 'any Protestants . . . here', suggesting that human favour (their desire not to incur the displeasure of others) may be the reason they do not convert.

That this sermon exists only in notes means that the careful use of language which is apparent in the Anglican sermons is hidden from the modern reader. The references to lives of the saints presumably allude to *exempla* which Newman would have developed for the benefit of his hearers. They correspond to the many Scriptural references with which the Anglican sermons are replete. With those earlier sermons, Newman's method is essentially the same. He identifies a problem (e.g., 'the tyranny of fashion'). He identifies, or invites his congregation to identify for themselves, the hearers' position in relation to the problem. He holds before the congregation some truth of Christian faith which answers the problem, and he challenges them to accept it and to perform the practical actions which are implied in it. Newman's sermons 'were always practical in intent'[41] and the intent was to make his congregation better Christians. But in order to do that, they had to believe not only that it was possible but that it was desirable. 'Newman puts his finger on the central reason why Christians are not better than they are: They do not want to be.'[42] They did not want to be because they were insufficiently persuaded of the eternal consequences of their temporal actions; in brief, most Christians were simply too worldly.

Newman's sermon on 'The Greatness and Littleness of Human Life'[43] takes this as its theme. The problem is contained in the dying words of Jacob in Genesis 47. How can a man who has lived to be 130 complain that his days have been few? asks Newman. Because, he answers, human capabilities are greater than the span of life allocated to us, however long we live. The reason is that we are made to be immortal but live with mortality. Having laid out this challenging thesis, Newman then has to lead his hearers

---

41 Vaughan, *op. cit.*, p. 39.
42 Ker, *Selected Sermons*, p. 46.
43 *Parochial and Plain Sermons*, vol. 4, pp. 214–25.

through an understanding of how to deal with it. They can recognize the issue, although it is one which does not often command their attention. The exceptions are when a person dies, especially when a younger person dies, even more especially when a younger and saintly person dies. Newman increases the tension between the idea of immortality and the fact of mortality (for which he finds echoes in the Old Testament) by asking the congregation to consider their own mortality. From the perspective of life's end they will see how little a thing it is. The gospel truth which is addressed to this is that life has value (Newman maintains *only* has value) as the field in which we are able to meet with God and his saints on earth and as preparation for life everlasting. But Newman is aware that he has unsettled his audience here and he identifies himself with their discomfort. They and he may not be as enthusiastic as he thinks they ought to be to exchange this life for another. They do not cry 'Come, Lord Jesus'. The reason is their consciousness of their guilt. The challenge is simply to long for and to pray for the forgiveness that makes mortals fit for the immortality for which they are intended.

'*Cor ad cor loquitur*' ('heart speaks to heart') was Newman's motto. The power of his preaching, as his contemporaries witnessed, was that he spoke the truths that he had discovered for himself. Lischer may be right that it was Schleiermacher who 'single-handedly reinvented the sermon as a medium through which the speaker imaginatively imparts his or her own experience of God to those who are receptive to it',[44] but Newman was not far behind him. That he had wrestled with the issues which he laid before his auditory was obvious; in some ways he anticipated the approach of the late twentieth-century homileticians in that he takes the congregation along with him as he re-enacts his own journey of faith. Always in a Newman sermon the listener is made aware of the disconnection between his or her own faith and the wonders of the gospel; the disturbance is deliberate: 'to be at ease, is unsafe'.[45] Almost always in a Newman sermon

44 R. Lischer (ed.), *The Company of Preachers: Wisdom on Preaching, Augustine to the Present*, Grand Rapids, Michigan and Cambridge, UK: Eerdmans, 2001, p. 8.

45 *Parochial and Plain Sermons* I, pp. 41–56.

that disturbance is achieved not by its being forced on the congregation with powerful rhetoric or force of argument, but by the hearer being gently yet irresistibly led to it. When that point is reached, the attractive but uncompromising demands which are implicit in it are laid before the congregation; the choice is always the same – the deceptive delights of the world or the discipline of obedience that leads to freedom.

> Let us turn to the living and true God, who has revealed Himself to us in Jesus Christ. Let us be sure that He is more true than the whole world . . . and if we doubt where the truth lies, let us pray . . . Him to give us humility, that we may seek aright; honesty, that we may have no concealed aims; love, that we may desire the truth; and faith, that we may accept it . . . Let us be filled with one wish – to please God; and if we have this, I say it confidently, we shall no longer be deceived by the world.[46]

The first person is both deliberate and natural. Here was a preacher who was journeying into the deep truths of the faith, and was inviting his hearers to join him in the quest.

This is utterly typical of Newman's approach to preaching. Early in his career, Newman compared preaching to writing a letter,[47] at a time, significantly, before Rowland Hill had introduced the penny post. A letter then (unlike the email of today) was a thing of substance; one did not write unless there was something significant to be said and the writing of a letter therefore demanded considerable time and effort. Each of Newman's sermons was an 'earnest letter' from the Church to the believer. Progress through the sermon was linear, from the point where the Church effectively greeted the listener to the point when the preacher was silent and the Church awaited a reply.

Newman's sermons 'are not', in E. T. Vaughan's view, 'in all respects safe or even possible models for other men to copy'.[48]

---

46 Ker (ed.), *Selected Sermons*, p. 366.
47 Ellison *op. cit.*, p. 84.
48 'Newman as a Preacher', p. 44.

The present writer wishes to challenge the second part of that view and to suggest that Newman's sermons are not only possible but also recommendable models for modern preachers. However, in attempting to demonstrate that, Vaughan's first objection needs to be taken seriously.

The form of a Newman sermon can be summarized as having five stages. Newman did not always deliver this entirely sequentially and sometimes parts of the sermon (often the first and second sections) are brought together, but almost invariably it is possible from the script or notes of a sermon to detect:

1 ('The Story') The element of tradition with which the sermon begins. This might be a biblical text or story or it might be an occasion that is being celebrated or an issue that is before him. The former is the usual pattern in the Anglican sermons; all three are to be found in the Catholic ones.
2 ('The Failure') A difficulty connected with the element of tradition. It might be that the demands appear at first sight to be onerous or unreasonable or it might be that the item of faith is often disregarded.
3 ('The Recognition') An assertion that this is not a general issue. It is specific to the life of the auditor who is brought to recognize this.
4 ('The Opportunity') A promise that the gospel has provided the means to resolve any dissonance between the experience of the listener and the demands of tradition.
5 ('The Challenge') The hearer is invited to accept the grace of God that is offered, but has to recognize that grace is not cheap and demands obedience.

The crucial section is the third. The listeners are invited to see for themselves that their doubts are being addressed, their sins are being condemned or their lukewarm faith being held up to examination. For the form to have any power, the preacher needs to have made assumptions about those who are listening and have made those assumptions correctly; this is where Vaughan's word of caution needs to be heard. Newman himself warned that a preacher should be quite sure that he understands the persons he is addressing before he ventures to aim at what he considers to be their ethical condition; for, if he mistakes, he will probably be doing harm rather than good. I have known consequences to occur very far from edifying, when strangers have fancied they knew an auditory when they did not, and have by implication imputed to them habits or motives which were not theirs. Better far would it be for a preacher to select one of those more general subjects which are safe than risk what is evidently ambitious, if it is not successful.[49]

Part of Newman's method was often gently to bring his subject closer to the listener, by identifying a failure of those outside the church but then demonstrating that many in the pews (himself often included) were not immune.

A Newman sermon has a single idea and its aim is to drive that idea deep into the heart of the listener. The image of a nail being hammered into a wall or (an analogy which Charles Simeon used) a screw being fixed in a place is a good one and implies both the advantages and the risk of this approach. Despite the deceptively gentle tone that he adopts, Newman's sermons can strike deep, and as he recognized, to strike deep in the wrong place can be pastorally catastrophic. There can be a thin line between the proper exercise of a preacher's responsibility to awaken in the hearers a consciousness of sin and the effect of leaving the congregation falsely accused. One of two outcomes might follow if the line is crossed. The preacher's own ministry can be undermined as indignant congregants refuse to accept the relevance of the analysis in other matters to themselves or (which is worse) a sensitive soul who is consciously striving to work out his or her salvation can suffer from the corrosive effects of unmerited guilt. Pastoral knowledge of the congregation and (as Newman had) a sound understanding of psychology are the necessary prerequisites for this form of preaching.

As are the preacher's devotions. It is a commonplace amongst those who advise preachers that prayer must be a preliminary

---

49 *Idea of a University*, p. 419.

to any sermon preparation. Kenton Anderson argues that different approaches to preaching demand correspondingly different uses of prayer,[50] and while that is true it may also be the case that some forms of preaching make greater demands on the preacher's spiritual resources than do others. It is also a commonplace that serious theological study is indispensable in sermon preparation, and again it is arguable that some forms of preaching require greater exegetical or doctrinal spadework than others. Newman's approach was predicated upon prayer and reading. His rule of life in 1842 was such that he allocated out of each day four and a half hours to his devotions and twice that amount of time to study.[51] The man who could 'tell people things about themselves they did not know until then'[52] had been the equivalent of a whole day on his knees and two at his desk since last he spoke to them.

Granted that detailed meditation on both the resources of faith and the human condition lie behind it, can a preacher still use the Newman form? It is not necessary to share Newman's theology (which in many of the sermons seems to imply a pessimism about the possibility of his hearers working out their salvation) to adopt (and to adapt) his method, though the form will only work if it concludes with a challenge that the congregation can recognize as appropriate and acceptable. 'Newman came into the pulpit just when people felt the discontent but had not quite expressed it. He articulated what they felt.'[53] Allied to good pastoral practice, preaching should be addressing that felt but unvoiced discontent. The preacher will need to have asked not only 'To whom am I writing this letter?' but also, 'Why am I writing this letter?' and 'What response am I looking to receive?' The questions could be addressed in either order. The 'why?' may be provided by the biblical text or the occasion and probably by a combination of the two. The looked-for response may be suggested by a situation in the Church or in the world but

---

50 *Choosing to Preach*, Grand Rapids: Zondervan, 2006, pp. 141, 168.
51 Martin, *op. cit.*, p. 71.
52 *Sermon Notes*, p. xx.
53 Chadwick, *Newman*, p. 19.

will in some way require the person addressed to adopt a lifestyle more authentically Christian.

An example might be that the preacher wants to address the issue of reading the Scriptures and to encourage the congregation in the discipline of daily Bible study. The thought might be prompted by an occasion (a sermon for Bible Sunday, for example) or by a pastoral awareness that this is an area of devotion absent from many of the congregants' lives. Alternatively, the theme may be suggested by the text appointed for the day. The ways that Newman used Scripture in his preaching were manifold. A sermon (particularly from his Anglican period) would be full of references, sometimes merely allusive and sometimes developed. On occasions he would take one text as his starting point but end triumphantly on another[54] or he would interpret one text by reference to another.[55] In this case, the modern preacher shaping a sermon in this fashion begins with 2 Kings 22.1–9.

1 The story of the finding of the scroll in the temple and the subsequent reform can be related by the preacher. Here was a nation called back to God and reshaping its own life around Torah – God's Word to them.

2 The failure of people to live in response to what is read in the Scriptures is not unique to the people of Judah before Josiah's reforms. Ignorance of the Bible can become a feature of the life of a nation at any time and the moral life of a society disintegrates because of it. The preacher may want to illustrate this point with biblical and/or historical examples.

3 The recognition could be presented in three stages:

3.1 Widespread biblical illiteracy in contemporary society is easily illustrated. Anecdotal evidence of schoolchildren not knowing Gospel stories, quiz contestants failing to name correctly all (or any) of the four evangelists, or the misquotation

---

54 For an example of this technique, see *Parochial and Plain Sermons*, vol. 8, pp. 185–200.

55 As in his sermon on the parable(s) of the two sons, *Parochial and Plain Sermons*, vol. 3, pp. 102–113.

of recognizable phrases ('turn the other cheek', 'go the extra mile') are plentiful.

3.2 The preacher can then demonstrate that (to a significant if lesser degree) this biblical illiteracy is to be found in the churches, because many church members are poorly acquainted with their Bibles (a point that could be illustrated with research statistics which is probably a better option than using anecdotes which could be too close to the listeners' own experience at this stage).

3.3 The preacher then invites the hearers to be honest with themselves about their own familiarity with the Scriptures. This might be done through a series of rhetorical questions on less commonly read passages; for example, can they name Abraham's second wife or tell each other anything at all about (or even spell) Habakkuk? The questions might then ask about passages more obviously central to everyday Christian practice; for example, how familiar are the congregation with the Sermon on the Mount?

4   The opportunity picks up the issue from part 3 and discusses examples of groups and individuals whose lives have been shaped by their deep knowledge of Scripture. These could be biblical or from Christian history. This section might end with reference to Augustine's *Confessions* and relate the important moment when he heard a voice saying 'Tolle et lege' ('Pick up and read').[56]

5   The challenge (particularly in a Eucharist) reminds the congregation that they claim to be an Easter people and that Christ walks with them. This links to the story of the Emmaus road. Christians can hear the Lord opening the Scriptures to us (the use of the first person at this point is appropriate as Newman recognized) and our hearts can burn within us, but only if we have some initial idea what it is he is talking about. And then, Christ vanishes from the disciples' sight. What we do next is up to us. The letter has been delivered; the reply is awaited.

---

56 *Confessions*, Book VIII (tr. E. B. Pusey, *Confessions of Saint Augustine*, London: Nelson, 1938, ch. 12).

7

WILLIAM EDWIN SANGSTER

The Last of the Great Entertainers?

In a brief history of Christianity edited by Christopher Howse, there is a reproduction of a painting of 1880 by Walter Frederick Roofe Tyndale. It shows a congregation sitting attentively in pews and is titled 'The Sermon'. Below the picture, the caption reports that at that date 'an unfeigned taste for hearing sermons was still surprisingly common'.[1] Was Anthony Trollope, then, in a minority? His frequently quoted objection to the 'preaching clergyman' with his 'power of compelling an audience to sit silent, and be tormented' rings as a heartfelt plea against some of the sermons that Trollope must have heard.

> We are not forced into church! No; but we desire more than that. We desire not to be forced to stay away. We desire, nay we are resolute, to enjoy the comfort of public worship; but we desire that we might do so without an amount of tedium which . . . is the common consequence of common sermons.[2]

Trollope's grievance seems to have been the sense that the Anglican clergymen of his day felt obliged to deliver a sermon on every

---

1 *AD: 2000 Years of Christianity*, London: SPCK, 1999, pp. 162f.
2 *Barchester Towers*, London: Hamlyn, 1987, p. 47.

possible occasion. Most of them, if Trollope is to be believed, simply were not up to the task; though that did not mean that all were not. The problem may even have been that some preachers were worth hearing and those with lesser gifts were attempting to imitate them. It was, perhaps, not sermons *per se* to which the novelist was objecting but indifferent ('common') sermons. If so, the phenomenon was hardly a new one:

> There must be preachers if we look to be saved. I told you of this gradation before in the tenth to the Romans; consider it well. I had rather ye should come of a naughty mind to hear the word of God for novelty or for curiosity to hear some pastime than to be away. I had rather ye should come as the tale is by the gentlewoman of London. One of her neighbours met her in the street and said, 'Mistress, whither go ye?' 'Marry,' said she, 'I am going to St. Thomas of Acres to the sermon; I could not sleep all this last night, and I am going now thither; I never failed of a good nap there.'[3]

So Hugh Latimer encouraged the congregation at the court of Edward VI to take preaching seriously as a part of their worshipping lives. Latimer's contemporary at St Thomas of Acre might have had his congregation dozing, but it is unlikely that Latimer himself ever did. His direct speech and occasionally vulgar language, his profusion of good stories and humorous illustrations, and his passion for his subject made the Bishop of Worcester one of the most popular preachers of his day. He was not, of course, the first preacher to gain a personal following, but he stands at the head of a tradition in Britain which lasted until the mid-twentieth century and still can be seen in some parts of the Church, particularly in the nonconformist denominations. It was a tradition of, in effect, inviting people to an act of worship in order that they might hear a particular preacher. A popular preacher, a preacher with a reputation for offering a lively or edifying sermon, could 'pull a crowd'. According to Caroline

---

3 Latimer, 'Sixth Sermon before Edward VI', in O. C. Edwards, *A History of Preaching*, vol. 2, Nashville: Abingdon Press, 2004, p. 302.

Richardson, it was Samuel Pepys who, in the seventeenth century, 'made church-going an art and sermon-tasting a pleasure'.[4] The diary is littered with references to the sermons that he heard and with his, sometimes uncomplimentary judgements upon them. But Pepys was only reflecting the interests of his day. The preacher he most esteemed was Robert Frampton (who was later to become Bishop of Gloucester) and apparently Pepys was not alone. On Sunday 20 January 1667, Pepys tells us,

> I [went] to church, and there, beyond expectation, find our seat, and all the church crammed, by twice as many people as used to be: and to my great joy find Mr. Frampton in the pulpit; so to my great joy I hear him preach, and I think the best sermon, for goodness and oratory, without affectation or study, that ever I heard in my life. The truth is, he preaches the most like an apostle that ever I heard man; and it was much the best time that ever I spent in my life at church.[5]

It would appear that Frampton was not alone in being able to draw a crowd. Other popular preachers of the late seventeenth century included Edward Stillingfleet, Robert South, Thomas Fuller and John Tillotson.[6] Sermons were printed, and Pepys also tells us of evenings that he spent discussing the works of Stillingfleet, but the live event was far more popular.[7]

Fashions change, as we have seen; by the mid-eighteenth century the disciples of Tillotson were no longer the attraction their master had been, and the popularity of the pulpit seems to have waned somewhat, until the general view was that to attend a sermon in the eighteenth century meant to subject oneself to a lecture on morals and little else[8] (hence, in part at least, the early popularity of Howell Harris, Whitefield and Wesley). The name of Whitefield, in particular, was able to rival other attractions in

---

4 C. Richardson, *English Preachers and Preaching 1640–1670: A Secular Study*, London: SPCK, 1928, p. 25.

5 R. G. Braybrooke (ed.), *Diary and Correspondence of Samuel Pepys* <www.bibliomania.com> 1666–67, p. 3.

6 Richardson, *op cit.*, p. 32.

7 Richardson, *op. cit.*, p. 47.

8 C. d'Haussy, *English Sermons: Mirrors of Society*, Toulouse: Presses Universitaires du Mirail, 1995, p. 30.

the capital, with reports of his dramatic abilities causing actors to attend his sermons just to admire his technique.[9] Whitefield's American preaching missions were attended by thousands (and possibly no one in the history of the Church had preached to so many before Whitefield); in Britain he was the subject of both adulation and lampoonery. However, the itinerant (and often open-air) preaching of the evangelical revival stands, in a sense, outside of the tradition of popular preaching in which people chose their Sunday place of worship because of the preacher. By the mid-nineteenth century, that tradition was very much in evidence once again; sermon-tasting was back in fashion. In the 1830s, a visitor to London could find a guide listing where the most respected of preachers of the day were to be heard, implying that the Sunday sermon was one of the many tourist attractions the capital had to offer.[10] Later in the century, people would set out specifically to hear Spurgeon, Lyddon or Dale. The revivalists also had their followers, but the popularity of Moody or William Booth was matched by that of Anglican and nonconformist ministers in their regular pulpits. There were Victorians who valued good preaching and went out of their way to find it; in 1884, the *Spectator* attempted to survey opinion as to who the best preachers were. It was a curiously limited piece of research, both in design (the preachers had to be 'English-speaking Protestants') and in execution (most of the respondents were themselves clergy and the numbers of votes did not exceed a few hundred), but the very fact that it was conducted demonstrates the high esteem in which the general public still held the preacher's craft.

Faith in that esteem continued into the mid-twentieth century. W. E. Sangster could maintain as late as 1954 that a good preacher would always be able to find a congregation.

If [a minister] comes to [preaching] aware of his awful privilege and open to the endowments which God gives to those he calls, his church may not fill, but his people will be blessed . . .

---

9 Edwards, *op. cit.*, vol. 1, p. 435.
10 d'Haussy, *op. cit.*, p. 23.

Such a man will not lack hearers. The rumour of his faithfulness and God's power will go abroad, and the hungry sheep will gather and be fed.[11]

Fifty years after that was written, opinions are divided as to whether such assurance was justified. Fifty years before it was published, the comment would have been indisputable.

Sangster believed that there was a spiritual interpretation of the phenomenon of the popular sermon. 'People both need and want the Word of God.'[12] But people also want (and perhaps need) to be entertained. Highmindedly, Sangster resisted the notion fiercely. 'No one who takes this high view of preaching could ever think of it as entertainment.'[13] It is a debatable sentiment. Latimer took a high view of preaching; the whole thrust of the sixth sermon was to shame his brother bishops into taking their homiletical ministry seriously, yet he clearly intended to entertain. Whitefield regarded his preaching as discharging a sacred mission and was vehement in his opposition to the theatre,[14] but there was something theatrical about Whitefield. A famous anecdote tells of his so dramatically relating the tale of a blind man walking too close to the precipice when preaching in front of the Countess of Huntingdon that one of her guests leapt up and shouted, 'Good Lord! He's gone!'[15] The evidence from the nineteenth century clearly points to preaching being understood as a form of entertainment,[16] and when the architects of Methodism's Forward Movement were commissioned at the end of that century to build the central halls, they manifestly interpreted their commissions as to produce venues to rival the music hall or theatre. This was the age in which preachers took trouble to advertise their sermons. A reader of a London Saturday newspaper in the 1890s would be able to see on what John Clifford or Hugh Price Hughes intended to preach the next morning. The fame of preachers spread over-

---

11 *The Craft of Sermon Construction*, London: Epworth Press, 1954, p. 27.

12 *op. cit.*, p. 27.

13 *op. cit.*, p. 16.

14 J. Downey, *The Eighteenth-Century Pulpit*, Oxford: Clarendon Press, 1969, p. 184.

15 Downey, *op. cit.*, p. 171.

16 d'Haussy, *op. cit.*, p. 23.

seas. 'So many were the American visitors to the City Temple that Parker declared that the pews at the back stretched to the Rocky Mountains.'[17] Horton Davies quotes Thomas Burke's account of aunts coming 'with news of a wonderful preacher heard at some outlying church, in the manner of an impresario reporting to the opera-directors on a new Wotan'.[18]

The apogee of this trend can be taken to be Charles Haddon Spurgeon (1835–92). The 'boy preacher' initially gained the sort of renown that Mozart did for a talent remarkable for his years, before developing into arguably the most widely read preacher of the age. He was only 17 when invited to the pulpit of Water-beach Baptist Chapel in Cambridgeshire, where he is reported to have increased the congregation from a matter of a few loyal attendees to 400 within a year. His fame spread and he was still in his teens when he was appointed to the New Park Street Baptist Chapel in London. Again, the numerical growth was prodigious and rapid. When his congregation outgrew the 800-seat building in New Park Street, the Metropolitan Tabernacle was constructed to accommodate seven times that number and to be filled twice every Sunday. Despite the brevity of his own formal education and his lack of theological training, Spurgeon began to teach others to preach and established his Pastors' College. His ministry was remarkable in a number of respects, but his sermons continued to be the main reason for the reverence in which he was held. Not only was his delivery of a sermon 'one of the foremost tourist attractions in London',[19] his sermons were quickly, and widely, made available in print. Like Whitefield, Spurgeon had a reputation for his oral technique which actors would envy and imitate.[20] Like John Chrysostom, Spurgeon revised the transcript of a stenographer before allowing his sermons to be published, though unlike Chrysostom, the publication took place

17 Horton Davies, *Varieties of English Preaching 1900–1960*, London: SCM Press, 1963, p.18.

18 *op. cit.*, p. 18.

19 R. H. Ellison, *The Victorian Pulpit: Spoken and Written Sermons in Nineteenth-century Britain*, London: Associated University Presses, 1998, p. 58.

20 C. Skinner, in W. H. Willimon and R. Lischer (eds), *Concise Encyclopedia of Preaching*, Louisville: Westminster John Knox Press, 1995, p. 451.

the following morning in newspapers circulating as far away as Australia and the United States of America.[21]

There is no suggestion of a pejorative judgement in calling this tradition of preaching 'entertainment'. The word, of course, has more than one meaning. In the sense that to entertain means 'to provide (someone) with amusement or enjoyment', Sangster's rejection of the term is understandable. In its second sense, 'to receive (someone) as a guest and provide them with food and drink',[22] to entertain is precisely what Sangster, Spurgeon and many others were doing from the mid-nineteenth to mid-twentieth century. John Stott might be said to be a late exemplar of the preacher as entertainer, but like Sangster he resisted the idea and expressed his disgust at the (now defunct) practice of sermon-tasting, as 'a reprehensible kind of ecclesiastical pub-crawling'.[23] The distinction is between the equivalent of sermonic fast food and the substance of Christian teaching. The ministry of Spurgeon (or Lloyd-Jones, Stott, Weatherhead, Parker, Dale, or Hugh Price Hughes) was consciously conceived as being to invite 'sinners to the gospel feast' and to nourish them with food from the Scriptures. It is in the context of that tradition that the homiletic ministry of William Edwin Sangster has to be understood. Although his writings on the construction and illustration of the sermon became the text books for preaching in a number of ministerial training establishments, they might have been as much the theory for a method whose day was passing as a guide for future practitioners.

Sangster was renowned as a preacher throughout the years of his ministry in the Methodist Church. He was accepted as a candidate for ordination shortly before he was demobilized from the army at the end of the Great War (without having consciously offered himself) and quickly attracted notice for his ability in the pulpit.[24] His ministry in his third appointment (in Liverpool) was marked by what his colleagues called 'Sangsteritis', the practice

---

21 Davies, *op. cit.*, p. 18.

22 Both definitions from *The Oxford Dictionary of English*, 2nd edn, 2005, p. 579.

23 *I Believe in Preaching*, London: Hodder and Stoughton, 1982, p. 50.

24 P. Sangster, *Doctor Sangster*, London: Epworth Press, 1962, pp. 46–56.

of some churchgoers of passing other chapels in order to attend the one where Sangster was preaching, and his invitations to minister in Scarborough and in Leeds (where he replaced another immensely popular preacher, Leslie Weatherhead) were based on the assessment of his pulpit proficiency. The most public years of his ministry began in 1939 when (on the day war broke out) he commenced his ministry at Westminster Central Hall, 'the first pulpit in Methodism' according to his son and biographer.[25] So popular was the evening service in Sangster's day that when the Hall was requisitioned in 1945 for the first General Assembly of the United Nations, the trustees struggled to find a building large enough to accommodate the congregation, finally settling on the London Coliseum. Sangster continued at the Central Hall until his appointment as Secretary of the Methodist Home Mission Department in 1955, a role which caused him to travel, and to preach, more widely, but from which he was to retire early on grounds of ill-health. By 1959 he was 'a travelling preacher who can neither travel nor preach'[26] as muscular atrophy took hold. He died in 1960.

Sangster's importance in the history of preaching rests both on his own pulpit ministry and the homiletic writings which he left. The Sangster bibliography can be a little confusing; essentially there were four works which claim to be of homiletic instruction. *The Craft of Sermon Illustration* appeared in 1946; this slim volume is exactly what its title suggests, a book of guidance on how a sermon can be enriched by the use of appropriate illustrations and how preachers can ensure that they have the necessary material to hand. *The Craft of Sermon Construction* followed it three years later. The two works were subsequently bound as one volume entitled *The Craft of the Sermon*. The title of *The Approach to Preaching* is less straightforwardly a description of that book's contents. It consists of six addresses which Sangster gave to the students in British Methodist theological colleges in the year 1950–51 (when he served as President of the

---

25 *op. cit.*, p. 124.
26 *Westminster Sermons*, vol. 1: *At Morning Worship*, London: Epworth Press, 1960, p. iii.

Methodist Conference). They are more advice to ordinands than guidance about preaching; Sangster instructed the young men in every aspect of their calling from the need to get up in the morning to the inadvisability of smoking tobacco. His last work on homiletics, *Power in Preaching* (1958), was more specifically on the subject of the sermon, consisting of a number of lectures that he had delivered about preaching and intended to supplement *The Craft of the Sermon*. Sangster was curiously hesitant about publishing his own sermons. He referred to an early collection (*Why Jesus Never Wrote a Book*) as 'occasional addresses', and asked very late in his life that none of his sermons be published post mortem apart from the thirty-four from the Central Hall years which he edited into two volumes (*Westminster Sermons*). The reticence might have been explained by the fact that Sangster did not preach from a manuscript; he maintained that the printed text could not fully do justice to the oral event which had 'the plus of the Spirit'.[27]

To a lesser degree than *The Approach to Preaching,* the title of *The Craft of Sermon Construction* is also something of a misnomer. It might have been more appropriately called *The Craft of Sermon Preparation*. Sangster never saw what he called 'sermon architecture'[28] as a discrete area separate from other matters (such as the content of the sermon or the psychological approach adopted). Consequently, sermon structure only merits one chapter in the book, sandwiched between his discussion of what is preached ('Sermons Classified According to Subject Matter') and how the congregation is to be reached ('Sermons Classified by Psychological Approach'). It would be erroneous to infer that Sangster placed little stock by sermon structure; for him it was absolutely vital for the method of preaching that he adopted and recommended. After the hours of preparation, the structure was what went with him into the pulpit.

No man need (or ought!) to burden his mind with memorized words. If the thought is clear, adequate words can be

---

27 *Westminster Sermons*, vol. 1, p. ix.
28 *Craft of Sermon Construction*, p. 64.

commanded in the moment of utterance . . . but the thought must be clear and the path plainly in view.[29]

In *The Craft of Sermon Construction,* Sangster offers five paths for a preacher to follow, although the first of his five categories of sermon structure does not, as Sangster himself acknowledges, correspond in type to the other four.[30] He deals with expository preaching (which he subdivides into seven different ways in which a preacher might address biblical material); what defines this as a structural type is the aim, which is to explain the meaning of Scripture.[31] The preacher, Sangster argues, should not have to devise a structure for such a sermon; having decided in which of the seven ways the Scripture is to be approached, 'the explanation of word and clause is usually fixed by their order in the text or passage under examination'.[32] At one level, this approach is simplicity itself (though if Sangster was recommending a return to Postils, he is not explicit about that; neither is there an example of such in his published sermons). At a deeper level (at which Sangster expected a preacher to work) there is nothing at all simple about it. The hours of exegesis, background study and imaginative entering into the world of the text which he believed expository preaching demanded should make it clear to the preacher how the sermon was to be organized.

Few of Sangster's published sermons seem to meet the criteria he outlines here, perhaps because so many are also easily classified according to his other types. 'The Three Groans'[33] treats Romans 8.18–30 and invites the congregation to listen to the three verses in which Paul uses the word 'groan'; each idea (that creation groans, that we groan, that the Spirit groans in us) is illustrated is such a way that during the third section Sangster carefully moves the congregation towards a more positive note by referring to the ministry of nineteenth-century philanthropists

---

29 *Power in Preaching*, London: Epworth Press, 1958 pp. 62f.
30 *Craft of Sermon Construction*, p. 79.
31 *Craft of Sermon Construction*, p. 68.
32 *Craft of Sermon Construction*, p. 79.
33 *Westminster Sermons*, vol. 1, pp. 78–87.

'who heard the groan of God'. Thus (Sangster concludes) if we hear the three groans we shall come to realize that God's final word is 'not a groan, but joy'.

'Four Judgments on Jesus'[34] adopts another of Sangster's approaches to the Bible, that of using multiple texts.[35] A twenty-first-century preacher might hesitate here, as the relationship between the sermon and the act of worship of which it is a part has, in Britain at least, changed in many denominations since the 1950s, thanks to the influence of the liturgical movement. For Sangster's congregation (unless the service be one of Holy Communion), the sermon would have been the last major part of the morning or evening worship, to be followed only by a final hymn and a blessing. This ordering created an auditory distance between the reading(s) and the sermon, so that there would be no expectation that the sermon should necessarily address the lections heard earlier. A preacher could, therefore, take a text from elsewhere, or (as Sangster does here) take four texts. Whether or not he would announce all four at the beginning of the sermon is not clear. His argument is outlined in the introduction – Jesus was one of those people who provoked strong reactions in people, either positive or negative. John 10.20 ('he hath a devil') is such a negative reaction; John 7.12 a more admiring one ('he is a good man'), but is nonetheless inadequate; Matthew 16.16 ('You are the Christ') is a statement of personal faith (Sangster makes no attempt to explain what 'Messiah' might have meant to a first-century Jew), but the congregation is invited to go (as Sangster testifies he eventually went himself) from Peter to Thomas and to confess Christ as 'Lord and God' (John 20.28).

A third example of what Sangster called expository preaching is one of his picture sermons. 'The aim of the sermon is to make the picture still more living by revealing comment.'[36] 'The Hands of Jesus'[37] invites the congregation to meditate on their own hands and on the hands that Christ showed to Thomas

---

34 *Westminster Sermons*, vol. 1, pp. 38–47.
35 *Craft of Sermon Construction*, p. 70.
36 *Craft of Sermon Construction*, p. 78.
37 *Westminster Sermons*, vol. 1, pp. 88–95.

(John 20.25). They were the hands of a working man, they were tender hands (which healed people), and they were the hands that were nailed to a cross. Those hands, Sangster concludes, are still lifted to bless, and continue their work through the hands of the congregation.

One might want to question whether any of these three is really expository preaching as that term is commonly understood. For all that they are thoroughly biblical, the driving force in the structure still seems to be the needs of the congregation rather than the exegetical matter of the text. For Sangster, structure was a blessing both to the preacher and to the congregation and the purpose of varying sermon structure was to avoid monotony among the hearers.[38] Those sermons which appear to correspond to his idea of 'expository' as a structure also correspond to others of his categories, while it is difficult to identify a Sangster sermon that might not be called 'expository', so central is the unfolding of the Bible's meaning to his whole homiletic ministry.

Three of the remaining four categories of structure that Sangster proposes are more clearly models of organizing material. The last is one which Sangster recommends only with caution. Some sermons are analogies;[39] the dominical discourses ('I am the Good Shepherd') might fit this group, as might some apostolic teaching ('You are the Body of Christ'), but it has, in Sangster's eyes, many dangers in the hands of lesser authorities. There is no example of his using it in the published sermon and his discussion is frustratingly brief. It may have been a common form in the ministries of some of his contemporaries, and to a degree the structure is implied by the title that might be used. The auditors of a sermon on 'Life as a Voyage' would expect there to be divisions – the embarking, the days without sight of land, the storms, the safe arrival, etc.[40] It is a structure which stands at the opposite end of the spectrum to 'expository'. There the structure was dictated by the text; here it is dictated entirely by

---

38 *Craft of Sermon Construction*, pp. 62f.

39 *Craft of Sermon Construction*, pp. 98f.

40 'Life as a Voyage' is a title Sangster proposes (*op. cit.*, p. 68). Quite what the divisions of 'The Devil as a Bowler' would be is more difficult to envisage.

the preacher's imagination. Sangster does not seem to have been truly at home with either model.

He was far more comfortable using his other three. The first is 'Argument' – 'those [sermons] that lay down a thesis and spend themselves in proving it'.[41] In this most technical part of the book, Sangster explains that this can be done in two ways, either deductively (arguing from the universal to the particular) or inductively (from the particular to the universal). The aim of the first approach is to bring a general point to bear on the individual listener by clarifying the thesis and disposing of objections to it. An example of Sangster's method here is his sermon for Children's Sunday, 'He Has a Special Love for Little Children'.[42] His text is taken from Jesus' encounter with Peter in John 21 ('Feed my lambs'), which Sangster (without any explanation) takes to apply to the younger members (or potential members) of the Church. His argument is that as Christ commands it, children should be sent to Sunday School. The first part of the sermon proves by the use of Gospel references that Jesus 'was vitally interested in children'. The second part notes that the Church is struggling to continue his interest, and that the consequences of that are deleterious for both Church and society, as the decline in Sunday School attendance has been accompanied by a general ignorance of the Christian religion and a rise in juvenile delinquency. Three objections which parents have voiced to Sunday School attendance are then dismissed as nonsense, before Sangster concludes with a final plea to parents to allow the Church to 'feed the lambs'. There is no suggestion that the subject has been comprehensively addressed; more than three objections might have been put forward and disposed of, but that would have made the sermon too 'heavy'.[43] Sangster also follows his own advice to move from the weakest argument (that the decline in Sunday School attendance is the result of middle-class snobbery) to his strongest (that it is fallacious to suggest that ignorance is a cure for bigotry). Three arguments are enough; Sangster is adamant

---

41 *Craft of Sermon Construction*, p. 80.
42 *Westminster Sermons*, vol. 2, pp. 120–8.
43 *Craft of Sermon Construction*, p. 87.

that the argumentative sermon must still be a sermon and not a ruthless destruction of opposition: 'to help people is the aim even more than the logical completeness of the argument'.[44]

To illustrate his notion of an inductive argument, Sangster refers to one of his own sermons, 'The Pain of Answered Prayer'.[45] It is not the easiest of his sermons, based on a text from the first part of Isaiah 21 (according to Gene Tucker, 'one of the most difficult passages to understand in the book')[46] which Sangster reads as Isaiah seeing a vision of future suffering. The message of the sermon is that God's light will show to those who pray the truth about themselves, however uncomfortable that truth may be. The sermon is a fine specimen of a preacher handling a complex spiritual topic, but it is not an example of inductive preaching as, for example, Fred Craddock would understand it.[47] Sangster's method is almost invariably deductive; he speaks from a position of authority. A possible exception is 'God's Law Is Not "On Approval"'.[48] Here Sangster takes a trivial incident, the fining of a man for not having a radio licence (a rule to which there could be no exception in the 1940s), and moves from it to argue that the Laws of God are similarly invariable. In each of the three sections, a particular limit to the notion of a universal law is considered (matters of will, place and time), but the divine precepts are shown to brook no such exception.

Sangster's next category of structure is what he calls 'faceting'.[49] The discussion in *The Craft of Sermon Construction* is surprisingly brief when one notices how many of Sangster's published sermons correspond to this model. Faceting is a word which Sangster 'borrowed . . . from the lapidary'.[50] It refers to the way

---

44 *Craft of Sermon Construction*, p. 87.

45 *Craft of Sermon Construction*, pp. 85f., *Westminster Sermons*, vol. 1, pp. 96–102.

46 'Isaiah', *New Interpreter's Bible*, vol. 6, Nashville: Abingdon Press, 2001, p. 185.

47 *As One Without Authority*, St Louis: Chalice Press, 4th edn, 2001, pp. 43–62.

48 *Westminster Sermons*, vol. 1, pp. 58–67.

49 *Craft of Sermon Construction*, pp. 89–92.

50 *op. cit.*, p. 89.

in which faces are cut onto a gemstone to enable it to reflect the light to its maximum benefit. The method suited Sangster's purposes particularly well. He notes that it is appropriate for 'how to' sermons,[51] and although he would use it also to illustrate a doctrine, it lent itself to the practical spirituality which Sangster was encouraging in his congregations. There were many ways in which a preacher could facet a text, and Sangster did not pretend to have explored all the possibilities. That is also true of many faceted sermons; Sangster will offer three or four 'faces' of the truth that he is expounding, but rarely more. The 'cutting' is only a part of the process in these sermons. The 'gem of truth' has first to be discovered. In the Palm Sunday sermon 'He Honours An Ass',[52] Sangster reflects on the use of a donkey at the entry into Jerusalem, and draws the conclusion that 'Christ has a use for [a person] . . . No matter how ordinary, ill-educated, disfigured, ill-born, one-talented or obscure a man or woman may be, Christ has a use for them.'[53] Those six adjectives then become the facets of the sermon. In 'Ambassadors for Christ',[54] Sangster bases his discussion on a recently published memoir by Lord Templewood, and relates four facets of Templewood's calling to the Pauline analogy in 2 Corinthians 5. Other sermons on this model take a biblical verse or picture and ask questions of it. His Easter sermon 'He Rises Again'[55] 'faceted' the stone at the tomb – 'What stone was rolled away?', 'Why was the stone rolled away?', 'What did the rolled away stone reveal?'

Sangster saw a clear distinction between 'faceting' and his next class, 'categorizing'.[56] Here the structure is dependent on the way in which the material of the sermon is broken, and usually the categories are self-limiting in number. Sermons for New Year's Eve will tend to be about time, a subject that naturally

---

51 *op. cit.*, p. 90.

52 *Westminster Sermons*, vol. 2: *At Fast and Festival*, London: Epworth Press, 1961, pp. 57–64.

53 *op. cit.*, vol. 2, p. 59.

54 *op. cit.*, vol. 1, pp. 103–13.

55 *op. cit.*, vol. 2, pp. 74–80.

56 *Craft of Sermon Construction*, pp. 92–8.

renders itself (as it does in Sangster's hands) into past, future and present.[57]

These sermons look remarkably similar to those that are faceted, as Sangster notes. The difference is in the approach of the preacher, though it might not be apparent to the listener. In 'faceting' the preacher can impose a structure on the sermon; with categorizing, the preacher infers it from the text or subject. So, presumably, Sangster would understand 'Ambassadors for Christ' as an example of faceting, while 'A Freeman of the City'[58] is structured by categories, as Sangster maintains that there are four (and only four) ways in which a person could acquire citizenship in ancient Rome, only one of which is analogous to the privilege of the citizenship of heaven.

Sangster's discussion of structural type only deals with the 'central architecture' of the sermon. A sermon *might* also require an introduction.[59] With his analogy of architecture, Sangster speaks (unoriginally) of the exordium as the porch to a house. It is, he asserts, an optional extra.[60] If one is to be used, its purpose should be to arrest the congregation's attention, and it should be kept brief, so as not to be out of proportion with what follows. It was advice that Sangster followed in his own preaching. While almost all of his published sermons have introductions, they are uniformly brief; one of the distinctive features of Sangster's prose was his terse and concise style. 'He expounded the central themes of Scripture in a breath-takingly rapid and succinct way.'[61] There is no unnecessary verbiage in Sangster, and therefore no leisurely journey to his starting point. If he cannot begin his discussion of the central theme immediately (as he does, for example, in 'They Which Receive Abundance of Grace'),[62] he sets out to do so as speedily as possible. His Passion Sunday sermon 'He is Lonelier than the Loneliest'[63] simply states what his theme is and then

---

57 *Westminster Sermons*, vol. 2, pp. 18–27.
58 *op. cit.*, vol. 1, pp. 124–33.
59 *Craft of Sermon Construction*, pp. 119–35.
60 *op. cit.*, p. 124.
61 Davies, *Varieties of English Preaching*, p. 205.
62 *Westminster Sermons*, vol. 1, pp. 68–77.
63 *Westminster Sermons*, vol. 2, pp. 47–56.

plunges into a discussion of the profound psychological sufferings of Jesus.

Conclusions, Sangster avers, are not to be treated in the same
way as introductions.[64] Here brevity can be a failing. He offers
a number of ways in which a sermon might be brought to its
'masterly finish', although not all are of equal value. His point
is that the sermon has to achieve something and that the conclusion must emphasize the aim. He rejects the notion of a 'peroration', understanding that word to mean a rhetorical flourish. A
conclusion had to be sincere and closely related to the content
of the sermon, and was not, in Sangster's view, strictly necessary; not all the published sermons have a conclusion as a separate section. His invariable rule of working towards his sharpest
point could render a peroration redundant. He often reinforced
this rule by summarizing the earlier points before beginning his
discussion of the final one. 'He Dies, He Must Die'[65] is unusual
in that it has two parts. The first is a detailed exposition of his
theme that the cross was not an incongruity but that sacrifice
is a part of all life. The second half argues that only a Saviour
who accepted suffering could reveal our sinfulness, free us from
sinfulness and meet us in suffering. And there it ends.

It is far from unusual to find a Sangster sermon that asks three
questions or makes three assertions. He recognized the power
of three although he, like most homileticians, did not claim to
be able to explain it.[66] What he rightly notes is that the use of
a threefold pattern is not in itself a structure; it might be that
a subject has three categories or that the preacher has given it
three facets, or it might be that the argument demands a thesis, antithesis and synthesis, or major premise, minor premise and conclusion. What he does not notice is that there is a
mnemonic strength in the number (which may simply reflect its
common use). Mnemonics did not interest Sangster. It was not
his practice to arrange his headings with alliterative or rhyming

---

64 *Craft of Sermon Construction*, pp. 136–50.
65 *Westminster Sermons*, vol. 2, pp. 65–73.
66 *Craft of Sermon Construction*, p. 100.

patterns.[67] 'My sermons are not to be remembered but trans-lated.'[68] What mattered was the difference that the sermon made to the lives of those who heard it, not the imprint that it left on their memories.

So is it unfair to speak of Sangster as 'a great entertainer'? He would have resisted the epithet, but it cannot be denied that he stood in the tradition of those whose ministry was to welcome people into the life of grace and to feed them with the Word of God and congregations flocked in order to be welcomed and fed. In one respect, his analysis of structure represented that whole tradition. His sermons imply an understanding (like Mel-anchthon's) of the preaching task which is primarily didactic. His insistence on the importance of illustration (arguably the area of his greatest strength as a homiletician) is reminiscent of Latimer. His semi-detached openings and integral conclusions echo Simeon. His view of structure as a device to confront his hearers with the Word of God is not unlike Spurgeon. But all were means to an end. Structure had to be varied in order that monotony be avoided. It was the impression that was made on his congregation that was his major concern and that he made an impression is undeniable; 50 years after his voice was silenced, those who heard him still recall the experience with wonder. Part of that wonder is that it is difficult to analyse how he achieved what he did. 'Of the hosts of people who heard him, few could explain why it was such a great experience.'[69] Sangster's solution to the mystery would have been a spiritual one. As an Armin-ian evangelical, Sangster laid great store on the importance of experience. A preacher spoke from personal Christian experi-ence or had nothing to offer. Before he could deal with sermon preparation directly in *The Craft of Sermon Construction*, Sang-ster felt obliged to discuss 'indirect preparation' – the preacher's devotional life.[70]

---

67 *Craft of Sermon Construction*, p. 92.
68 *Westminster Sermons*, vol. 1, p. vii.
69 *Doctor Sangster*, p. 279.
70 *Craft of Sermon Construction*, pp. 152–8.

Sangster's work is still widely read, and his patterns are followed by preachers to this day. As he himself noted, while structure is vital it needs to be considered alongside the psychological approach which is to be adopted. Of course, some of his notions seem outdated; would anyone now dare to assume that sermons on social issues could have a threefold division relating to the working, middle and upper classes?[71] But many of his principles about how a preacher's material can be arranged so that it can be received, comprehended and (above all) effective in the life of the listener are still proving their validity. They do so now with many other approaches asking for the student-preacher's consideration.

---

71 *Craft of Sermon Construction*, p. 93.

8

THE FORM CHANGES SHAPE

Preachers of the New Homiletic

W. Edwin Sangster died in 1960. In the same year, Leslie Weather-head preached his last sermon at the City Temple in London. Within a few years, it must have seemed as though the passing of those two giants of the pulpit had marked the end of an era. Sangster had had great confidence in the power of the sermon; if his confidence was shared by others, it did not long outlive him. By the 1970s there was discernible in parts of the western Church a lack of faith in the power of the ministry of preaching. Books appeared arguing that the day of the sermon was past. Churches which had rejoiced in having a strong pulpit ministry at the centre of their worship began to question the value of the sermon altogether. Homiletical literature of the last quarter of the twentieth century was in many cases a deliberate and conservative reaction to the crisis. The starting point for John Stott in *I Believe in Preaching* was what he saw as the lamentable state of pulpit ministry. 'In some places the sermon is reduced to an apologetic five minutes; in others it has been replaced by either a "dialogue" or a "happening".'[1]

---

1 *I Believe in Preaching*, London: Hodder and Stoughton, 1982, p. 50.

The obituary of preaching has been written many times in the history of the Church, as Colin Morris eloquently points out.[2] The death notice was premature before and, Morris maintains, it is now. But the fact that he himself chose to begin his monograph on preaching as performance with a discussion of the question, and the implication that there is something in preaching that needs to be revived, makes it clear that at the beginning of the twenty-first century the crisis of confidence has not been resolved. There is still (at least in the British Church) an uncertainty amongst many about the place and the value of preaching. Still (again, Morris is right) hundreds of thousands gather Sunday by Sunday to listen to sermons and find that there are still thousands of ordained and lay people who have struggled in the previous week to have something to say to them, but the world changed in the latter half of the twentieth century and the change (which is not yet complete) shook some of the easy assumptions about preaching. The nature of the change is complex, and the effect on preaching manifold and still in process, but four general observations can be made.

In Britain at least,[3] the first and most obvious cause for the crisis in confidence in preaching was the rapid decline in church attendance. After the Second World War, and especially after 1960, the number of those present at a weekly act of worship in Britain fell rapidly. The trend continued and accelerated into the twenty-first century; in 1980 the number of Britons in church each Sunday was approximately six million, or 11 per cent of the population; by 2005 it was only 4 million, which was less than 7 per cent of the population.[4] This decline was in line with other indicators of Christian allegiance. By 1970 the proportion of infants brought for baptism in the Church of England had fallen to below (what was then) the alarming figure of 50 per cent for the first time, and by 1980 to below 40 per cent, and

---

2 *Raising the Dead*, London: Fount, 1996, p. xi.

3 It is quite clear that there was also a crisis of confidence in North America, although the levels of Church attendance there have remained much higher than those in western Europe.

4 P. Brierley, *UK Christian Handbook: Religious Trends 5* Swindon: Christian Research, 2006, p. 3.3.

other Christian churches witnessed a similar reduction.[5] By the year 2000 55 per cent of infants were not brought for baptism in any Christian denomination.[6] The number of places of worship has been drastically reduced, as has the number of clergy. But neither of the latter two diminutions has been in proportion to the loss of members and attendees. The result has been that although there have been fewer preachers ministering in fewer buildings to fewer congregations, the number of faces that they see when they look down from the pulpit has, generally speaking, been smaller than the number they might have seen ten, 20, or 50 years previously. What is most debilitating for the confidence of the Church in Britain is the evidence that the trends are continuing. Total church membership is predicted to be only 5 per cent of the population by 2040, taking it below what Peter Brierley estimates to be the key 'critical mass' (the number of people needed to make a significant difference as an organization within society).[7]

The reasons for this trend are complex and not fully understood. There is some evidence that it relates to a decline in the number of those who profess a Christian faith. Opinion pollsters in 1965 reported that only 2 per cent of the population claimed to be atheist; by the end of the century, the figure had increased tenfold. There was also by that time an enormous gap between stated profession and practice; those who answered the 2001 census question on religion as Christian were ten times the number who admitted to attending worship regularly.[8] Many would identify changes in life patterns. Three factors have combined to create pressure on families to use weekends for the purposes of cementing their own unity – greater social mobility that has led to more adults living away from the place of their birth and childhood, a higher divorce rate that has led to more parents living separately from their children, and the fact that most families

---

5 A. Hastings, *A History of English Christianity 1920–1990*, 3rd edn, London: SCM Press, 1991, p. 603.

6 Brierley, *op. cit.*, p. 4.4.

7 Brierley, *op. cit.*, p. 12.4.

8 Church attendance was 7.6 per cent of the population, the number declaring themselves to be Christian 72 per cent. Brierley, *op. cit.*, p. 2.2.

own a car and are able easily to travel. The appearance of the television set in many homes has been blamed for providing people with an easily accessible form of entertainment (with the much-repeated assertion that the 1960s BBC's dramatization of *The Forsyte Saga* drew thousands away from evening worship). In some circles, the finger of blame has been pointed at those who now choose to attend the cathedrals of Mammon in the high street or the shopping mall, as the 1990s saw a relaxation of the (admittedly already widely ignored) Sunday trading laws, with the result that what had been a day of rest prescribed by statute is now the second busiest day of the week for retail activity.

It is not difficult to appreciate why these trends, already apparent in the 1960s, have caused such concern to preachers. The widening spaces in the pews indicated that the people did not want to listen to their sermons. What deepened the unease was the realization that the sermon might have been part of the reason for the spaces in the pews, that the underlying story might not have been simply that the laity were no longer so eager to hear a sermon that they made every effort to attend services, but that they were so eager not to hear a sermon that they made a deliberate decision to remain at home. Mervyn Willshaw suggested that, although at many times in Christian history 'much preaching has been, and is, just plain boring', there was a new realization by the 1980s. 'The uncomfortable truth is, *and this may be new,* that while good sermons are unlikely to fill churches, bad sermons will certainly empty them.'[9] Of course, the relationship between the decline in churchgoing and the quality of preaching was never simply that of effect to cause. Morris is right; that conclusion would be a 'grievous injustice'.[10] But to whatever degree poor preaching contributed to shrinking congregations, many factors seemed to conspire to give the impression that that was the case. At the moment in history when the political leadership of the country began to invite the electorate to see everything in

---

9 M. Willshaw, 'The Decline and Fall of Preaching' in Davies (ed.), *The Testing of the Churches 1932–1982: A Symposium*, London: Epworth, 1982, p. 178 (italics added).

10 *Raising the Dead*, p. xiv.

terms of market economics, the preachers realized that the product they had to offer simply wasn't selling and suspected that part of the reason was that the product was defective.

The second cause for that crisis in confidence was the wider *zeitgeist* of the post-war period. Changes in society reflected an underlying sense that the old certainties were no longer to be trusted. The far wider provision of state education after 1944 had resulted by the 1960s in a population far better informed and equipped to think for itself and therefore confident to challenge some of the assumptions of the past. The 1960s in particular were a period of the liberalization of thinking and of conduct in a number of areas. The watersheds have been commonly identified and often rehearsed. The *Lady Chatterley* trial of 1960 (with its risible quotation from the prosecuting barrister about servants and wives not reading the book) and the abolition of stage censorship in 1968, the availability of oral contraception from 1963 and the abortion act of 1967, and the decriminalization of homosexual acts in 1967, all signified a society with a far more relaxed view of sexual morality in particular. Along with that came a more vocal challenge to political establishment, as television brought closer the changes that were happening elsewhere in the world, among them the student-led riots in Paris in 1968 and the anti-war protests in the United States of America as the country became embroiled in Vietnam.

All of this had a debilitating affect on the confidence of the preachers. At the end of the nineteenth century, leading Free Church ministers such as Hugh Price Hughes or R. W. Dale had been able to protest against social change or legislation they thought reprehensible and their views had been respected. Towards the end of the twentieth century preachers (even of the Church of England) no longer had the standing to do that, and may even have been grateful that they did not, as in some instances it was not at all clear what the churches should be saying about these major issues. Parliament had relaxed the divorce laws in 1969; the number of decrees absolute that were issued rose immediately, so that the number of marriages dissolved in 1975 (approximately 120,000) was three times the figure of a decade earlier.[11] Should preachers choose to address this issue, what were they to say? That it was a good thing that the guilt-fixing, sordid evidence-gathering and downright dishonesty of the old system had gone, or that, whatever the law said, marriage in the Christian understanding was a lifelong commitment and divorce was incompatible with that? Homosexual couples were free after 1967 to be open about the nature of their relationship, but again the Christian community was (and still is) divided on whether this was something to be welcomed or regretted. The abolition of the office of the Lord Chamberlain was symbolic of a new freedom of expression in the arts and the media, but while Mary Whitehouse campaigned vigorously in the name of the Christian faith against some of the expressions of that liberty, others in the churches took the view that censorship was always a dangerous device.

The crisis of confidence was deepened because the dismantling of the old certainties was apparent in the Church's consideration of its own creeds. Those too young to remember its publication marvel that John Robinson's slim volume *Honest to God* shook the foundations of the Church in 1963, but apparently it did. Whether that was because (as Hastings maintained) it spoke to the feeling of the times,[12] because Robinson was a bishop (and therefore far more prominent than, for instance, the 'Soundings' group of 1962),[13] or because Robinson was a consummate media performer and was able to gain an audience for his views, remains a matter for debate. What is clear is that by making some of the insights of Tillich, Bultmann and Bonhoeffer accessible to ordinary readers, he suggested to many in the Church that what they had always believed was not what a bishop of the Church of England believed. For those who thought that preach-

---

11 National Statistics Online (http://www.statistics.gov.uk).

12 *History of English Christianity*, p. 538.

13 *Soundings* was a collection of ten essays, published by theologians who wanted to 'identify pertinent questions which needed to be explored' rather than provide certain answers (K. Hylson-Smith, *The Churches in England from Elizabeth I to Elizabeth II*, vol. 3, London: SCM Press, 1997, p. 230). *Soundings: Essays Concerning Christian Understanding*, ed. Alec Vidler, Cambridge: Cambridge University Press, 1962.

ing might provide a haven from the storm that seemed to have blown away the eternal verities, the effect of Robinson was to invite the storm to rage in the harbour of the pulpit and pew.

The crisis of confidence in preaching was deepened by the liberalization of the 1960s because it cast light on the achievements of preaching in the past, some of which were not to be judged kindly. This was particularly the case where the changes that were being experienced were the ending of oppression. The movement for women's rights gained strength in the 1960s and 1970s challenging churches which had almost universally maintained a male hierarchy even when (as only the smaller Free Churches did) they ordained women as ministers. As the progressive end of colonialism in Africa asked the white churches to review their own record on supporting the rights of black people, so a question mark came to be cast over the whole preaching enterprise. The crisis of confidence in preaching was felt keenly in the United States of America as some in the 'white' churches had to recognize their contribution to the injustices that the civil rights movement was challenging. So the wisdom of the whole preaching enterprise was once again brought into question. It could not be denied that some preachers had (perhaps unwittingly) abused their privileged position and contributed to the sufferings of the oppressed and if the new climate refused to place a preacher 'six feet above contradiction', it might be just as well. But Willshaw was right to say that 'if that is a healthy state of affairs in general, it puts the preacher under greater pressure'.[14]

There was a fourth element that contributed to the crisis of confidence. The way in which people communicated changed in the 1960s and has continued to change. The presence of a television set first in more and more homes and then in more and more rooms in each home contributed to a culture in which information was received in images as much as in words. Strangely, over the following 40 years, that has not contributed to a reduction in the number of words in circulation but rather an increase which, to many minds, has caused or has been caused by a debasement of the currency. Newspapers are an obvious example of this. The

---

14 'The decline and rise of preaching?' p. 178.

number of newspapers sold each day has fallen over the last 50 years. The size of the newspapers (the number of words that each contains) has increased. Forty years ago, Sunday papers could be delivered by a boy or girl on a bicycle. Today, the number of supplements with each means that they are more often transported on foot with some sort of trolley, and Saturday editions are imitating their Sunday counterparts. Large sections of each paper are transferred every weekend by the householder straight to the recycling bin, without consideration of the content beyond an understanding that it would never be read. Similarly, the computerization that has developed rapidly since the 1980s may not have delivered (as once was promised) the paperless office, but it has given the operator of each terminal access to countless millions of words through the internet, far more than the user can expect to read. Each word therefore counts for less than once it did, and that has had an effect on preaching. As early as the 1960s the increased visualization of information sharing had led to a perceptible decline in the willingness of the population to be influenced by rhetoric. Words had become cheap, and preachers were aware of it.

Barbara Brown Taylor has noted something far more worrying.[15] Words did not only become cheap in the second half of the twentieth century, they became untrustworthy. George Orwell's nightmare vision in *1984* has not remained entirely fictional. The meaning of words has been twisted to suit the purpose of the speaker. Taylor blames the consumer culture for this.[16] In their desperation to part the public from its money, advertisers and marketing gurus use superlatives as their default option. 'Only' prefaces any price, however high. 'Best ever deals' and 'lowest ever offers' are promised to those who read the commercials in the newspapers and the copywriters hope that the public will not take literally their assertion that these offers are 'incredible' or 'unbelievable'. It is not that we live in a Humpty Dumpty world where words mean whatever the user wants them to mean; it is

15 *When God is Silent*, Cambridge, Mass: Cowley Publications, 1997, pp. 1–40.

16 Taylor, of course, is American but elements of her analysis are applicable this side of the Atlantic.

that we live in a world of debased language in which hyperbole becomes an expected cover for a lack of meaning.

Taylor suggests that the necessary response of a preacher to this is to use words with economy, courtesy and reverence. By economy, she means that preachers should say only what they know to be true and then sit down. Courtesy, in her analysis, is the opposite of the coercion which is the purpose of much of the hyperbolic advertisers' language. By reverence, she intends that preachers should not attempt to say what is unsayable. Those three qualities are reflected in Taylor's own preaching in which she is able to bring out the challenge of the gospel with a gentleness of touch that has made her one of the most popular and widely respected preachers in the United States of America. As well as being economic, courteous and reverent in the use of words, Taylor is also deliberately homely. If the language of rhetoric has lost its power, if the language of the media is equivocal, if the language of the marketplace is not to be trusted, the preacher does well to resort to the one place where people still (on the whole) say what they mean and mean what they say. The crowds of Matthew's Gospel are, according to Taylor, 'a gimpy, twitching group'.[17] John the Baptist died believing that Jesus was 'a languid saviour'.[18] Jesus' Galilean mission was 'a failure'.[19]

Taylor can be understood as part of a movement which came to be known as 'the New Homiletic'. Although it is conventional to credit the publication in 1971 of Fred Craddock's first book on preaching with beginning the movement and setting the agenda for future discussion,[20] the term antedates that by two years[21] and the changes have been far more widespread and varied to be attributed to a single cause. It is possible to argue that many of the main themes of 'the New Homiletic' are to be found in

---

17 *The Seeds of Heaven: Sermons on the Gospel of Matthew*, 2nd edn, Louisville: Westminster John Knox, 2004, p. 12.

18 *The Seeds of Heaven*, p. 12.

19 *op. cit.*, p. 17.

20 See, e.g., Charles Cranwell's article in W. H. Willimon and R. Lischer (eds), *Concise Encyclopedia of Preaching*, Louisville: Westminster John Knox Press, 1995, pp. 93ff.

21 E. L. Lowry, *The Homiletical Plot*, expanded edn, Louisville: Westminster John Knox, 2001, p. 122.

H. Grady Davis' 1958 work, *Design for Preaching*. If Davis was ahead of his time, what Craddock did was to capture the mood of his day exactly. Even the title of his book, *As One Without Authority*, expressed what preachers felt. Craddock's argument was simple. The climate of the late 1960s was uncongenial to the deductive preaching that had been the mainstay of pulpit material for a long time. This he defined as 'stating the thesis, breaking it down into points or sub theses, explaining and illustrating these points, and applying them to the particular situation of the hearers'.[22] For all its history, this was, Craddock claimed, 'a most unnatural mode of communication, unless, of course, one presupposes passive listeners who accept the right or authority of the speaker to state conclusions that he then applies to their lives'.[23] It was clear by the late 1960s that such a presupposition was unwarranted. The solution, Craddock believed, was to change from a deductive to an inductive approach to the preaching task, that is to say that a sermon should move from 'the particulars of experience that have a familiar ring in the listener's ear to a general truth or conclusion'.[24] What Craddock saw as the older model left the auditory with a choice – take it or leave it. Increasingly, they were leaving it. Inductive preaching invited the auditory to share the preacher's journey towards the truth.

That this concurs with the urging of those like Barbara Brown Taylor for reverence is no coincidence. Craddock acknowledged that there were already moves away from the deductive, authoritarian approach in preaching at the time that he wrote. More generally, the suspicion with an approach to preaching that offered an answer before it asked the question was heard most vocally from the increasing number of women in ordained ministry and therefore in the pulpit.[25] While it would be wrong to general-

---

22 F. Craddock, *As One Without Authority*, rev. edn, St Louis: Chalice Press, 2001, p. 45.

23 *op. cit.*, p. 46.

24 *op cit.*, p. 47.

25 In fact the ordination of women has not always been matched by the appearance of women in the pulpit, as a disproportionate number of ordained women are in posts without a regular preaching ministry. Carol A. Miles, 'And your daughters shall prophesy: Preaching as Women's Work', *Insight* 2004, p. 11.

ize about contrasting 'male' and 'female' models of preaching, research has shown that there is a distinctly female approach to the task, though it is not easy to identify where precisely that distinctiveness lies, as Christine M. Smith discovered in her early studies.[26] Arguing that until the time of her own and her contemporaries' work homiletics was entirely a male discipline,[27] Smith has developed a forceful and eloquent case that women preachers typically do not structure their sermons; rather they craft them in a manner for which she believes the best metaphor to be weaving. This form of preaching does not, she maintains, set the preacher above or against the congregation; rather the preacher identifies with the people he or she serves and makes connections with their experiences and needs in order to show something of the beauty of God's purpose. She quotes William Schulz: 'a true sermon is a tapestry drawn from tradition, memory, conversations long forgotten, candor, courtesy, pain and passion, fresh insight and fresh metaphor, but all united'.[28]

Barbara Brown Taylor is one who 'weaves' rather than 'structures' a sermon. Or rather, what she does might be described as embroidering. It is far from a perfect analogy, and the verb might sound pejorative, but no such connotation is intended. An embroiderer will work on a faint picture of the final scene. The thread is sewn through the fabric, forth and back, forth and back. Taylor's technique is similar. She lays before the listeners her text. The needle of her discussion goes from one side of the text which might broadly be termed Scripture (so Taylor will discuss the context of the passage, the situation of the redactor, the background in first-century Palestine, etc.) through the text and out to the other side which might be described as experience (the life that she and her listeners share or might have shared). To change the image, Taylor has herself described this process as being 'like Cyrano de Bergerac in the pulpit, passing messages between two would-be lovers', though she never forgets that she

---

26 *Weaving the Sermon: Preaching in a Feminist Perspective*, Louisville: Westminster John Knox, 1989, p. 11.

27 *op. cit.*, p. 40.

28 *op. cit.*, p. 20.

also is one of the lovers of God.[29] Through this process, the picture of the text emerges in brighter colours. What also happens in embroidery, of course, is that the thread gets shorter each time – the field of the Bible and the field of experience are drawn together, until, as Taylor works with the text, the listeners find themselves in the picture that has been enhanced. Her sermon on Matthew 14.22–33 provides an example.[30] She spends most of her time on the Scripture side of the picture – she discusses Matthew's inclusion of the walking on the water in comparison to the other evangelists, the ancient belief about (and fear of) the sea, and the character of Peter. The other side of the tapestry is not ignored; throughout the lengthy (for Taylor) discussion of Peter's character she is consciously referring to common human experience. Peter's enthusiasm is sincere and 'achingly familiar'.[31] We come to the point where the disciples are in the boat and Jesus approaches. Because Taylor looks at the text for a moment from the other side, she sees how odd Peter's request to come to Jesus is; it is a request for his doubt to be removed. Once Peter is on the water, she explores common human experiences – learning to swim, making a speech – which ended in panic. Back we go to Peter and Jesus' critical words. Back to us, who hear the words in our own context and the similarity between the preacher's own doubt and Peter's is described. Then the needle goes through the text with an interesting question: suppose Peter had not sunk. The answer is that the story would have had no relevance to the preacher's own experience which she shares with her hearers. We are now close to the end. The thread is short and goes from one side of the picture to the other with rapidity. 'When *we* sink, as *Peter* does, as *we all* do'[32] then Jesus saves us. Scripture and experience are brought together in the final image. '[Jesus] returns us to the boat, where our companions grab us by the scruff of the neck and haul us aboard . . . The wind ceases, and the waves hush, and in the awesome silence of that night

---

29 *The Preaching Life*, Plymouth: Cowley Publications, 1993, p. 83.
30 'Saved by Doubt' in *Seeds of Heaven*, pp. 55–60.
31 *op. cit.*, p. 57.
32 *op. cit.*, p. 60, italics added.

becoming day, all of us who are in the boat together worship him, saying, "Truly, you are the Son of God.""[33]

Barbara Brown Taylor is one of a number of preachers who have developed forms of preaching which respond to Craddock's plea to work inductively. Craddock saw this as a rejection of Aristotelian rhetoric,[34] but one of the most influential preachers of the 'new homiletic' sees his system as having recovered something from the ancient Greek philosopher.[35] Eugene Lowry has been one of the main proponents of 'narrative' preaching. He argues that a sermon is not a 'thing' like a wall to be constructed piece by piece but an organism that has a life of its own and needs to develop rather than to be assembled.[36] In this he is following in the steps of H. Grady Davis for whom form and substance in sermons belonged together. In thinking about how to organize a sermon, Davis maintained, preachers had to identify the single idea which they were going to communicate and then allow it to find its own form. The task was never to impose a form on an idea, nor to create a form for the idea, but to let the form emerge naturally from the idea.[37] Lowry's attitude is very similar. Putting together a sermon is not, in Lowry's view, a matter of architecture (as he had been taught) but rather of art, and the particular art form that most closely resembles the sermon is the story. So a convincing sermon will be story-like in its form. That does not mean that it is a story; story sermons are preached by many modern practitioners,[38] but the parallel narrative or retelling of the story of the text is not what Lowry aims to do. His preaching is narrative in that its form can be analysed as a plot line.

The form (or 'sequence' as Lowry prefers) has become known as 'the Lowry loop'. The loop has five stages.[39] In the first stage, the

---

33 *op. cit.*, p. 60.

34 *As One Without Authority*, p. 45.

35 E. L. Lowry, *The Sermon: Dancing the Edge of Mystery*, Nashville: Abingdon Press, 1997, p. 54.

36 *The Homiletical Plot*, pp. 6ff.

37 H. Grady Davis, *Design for Preaching*, Philadelphia: Fortress Press, 1958, p. 79.

38 See, e.g., E. Steimle, M. Nierdenthal, C. Rice, *Preaching the Story*, Philadelphia: Fortress Press, 1980.

39 *The Homiletical Plot*, p. 26.

preacher sets out to 'upset the equilibrium' of the congregation. He or she has to establish that there is an issue that needs to be addressed, a problem to be solved or a puzzle to be resolved. In the second stage, the plot thickens as the preacher attempts to 'analyze the discrepancy' – why are things not as they should be? Having done that (which Lowry considers to be the most critical stage of the process),[40] the preacher moves on to 'disclose the clue to resolution'. This is the crucial moment of reversal in which the preacher opens the way for the congregation to hear the gospel. In stage four, the congregation is invited to 'experience the gospel'; the answer at which stage three had hinted is expounded. Finally, the congregation is invited to 'anticipate the consequences'; a new world has been envisaged, in which the disease that the preacher identified has been healed.

An example of Lowry's method is his sermon on Elijah on Mount Horeb, 'Listening to the Dark'.[41] He begins by recounting the previous part of the story, Elijah's triumph over the prophets of Baal, and points out that this is an unusual set of circumstances in that Elijah is running away from success rather than failure and his reaction is self-pitying and inconsistent. In the second part of the sermon, Lowry continues to tell the story of Elijah not hearing God in earthquake, wind or fire. Only then does he start to talk about contemporary Christian experience, but he does so in a way that deliberately deepens his auditory's unease by kicking away what the congregation believes to be its answer.

> You say, 'But don't you know that the place to wait for it isn't wind, an earthquake, or a fire, but in a still, small voice?' But this solution won't work for us. This is the bad news I bring to you. It doesn't work that way, because wherever we think the voice is, it's not. It just doesn't happen.[42]

The congregation is not likely to be comforted by his personal illustration, a childhood memory of being frightened when his brother plunged into darkness the basement in which they were playing.

---

40 *op. cit.*, p. 39.

41 Published online at <www.PreachingTodaySermons.com/loweuglistod>

42 'Listening to the Dark', p. 3.

The answer is disclosed in the next section, though it is not an easy answer. Starting from the experience of preachers struggling for inspiration, Lowry argues that the word we need to hear is to be found in the places that we are not looking; God may speak to people through seemingly unimportant parts of a sermon, not necessarily through the main points. The clue to resolution is contained in one word – mystery. God is not predictable, but far beyond human understanding. The good news (Lowry's fourth section) is that this mysterious God is with us, even in the darkness. The question whispered to Elijah is not 'What are you doing over *there*?', but 'Why are you *here*?' As in other Lowry sermons, the conclusion can be quite sudden. All Lowry has said previously is brought together in a final sentence: 'In whatever form – loud, soft, short, long – the voice will come. One way or another that voice will say, "Boo!" It will scare you out of your wits. It ought to.'[43]

Lowry's is one of a number of ways of preaching that shape sermons in a narrative fashion.[44] But narrative preaching is by no means the only option available to the modern homiletician. Much preaching is still offered deductively (Tom Long and Cornelius Plantinga note that the three-point sermon has stubbornly refused to die),[45] and David Buttrick has recommended an approach which sees the sermon as a series of moves across the field of consciousness.[46] Thomas Troeger, in contrast, understands the sermon as an image.[47] The range of homileticians who, over the last 50 years, have suggested ways in which the sermon should be shaped according to the shape of the text, or ordinary discourse, or modern communications, is immense. O. C. Edwards is probably right when he writes that 'there seem to be more forms of preaching today than in all previous Christian centuries put together', though whether that is simply because there are more Christians, more preachers and more sermons is

43 *op. cit.*, p. 7.

44 K. Anderson, *Choosing to Preach*, Grand Rapids: Zondervan, 2006, p. 186.

45 *A Chorus of Witnesses*, Grand Rapids: Wm Eerdmans, 1994, p. 165.

46 D. Buttrick, *Homiletic*, Philadelphia: Fortress Press, 1987, pp. 305–29.

47 O. C. Edwards, *A History of Preaching*, vol. 1, Nashville: Abingdon Press, 2004, pp. 815ff.

doubtful.[48] The latter part of the twentieth century saw preachers challenged to restate what a sermon is and the multiplicity of answers has resulted in a multiplicity of forms. What has also emerged has been a new understanding of the importance of the form of the sermon. The new homiletic in all its manifestations has worked from an assumption that forming a sermon is not about organizing pre-existing material for the preaching event but is a process that is inseparable from the content and the context of the sermon. Again, Davis led the way: 'substance and form are two parts of the same thing'.[49] The objective of rhetoric from ancient time was to ensure that an utterance be carefully structured in order that what is said is clear; most of the preachers discussed in this book used the form or structure of their preaching in order to say something. Modern homileticians expect their sermons not only to say something but also to do something; the sermon is more experiential than expository.[50]

An intriguing model based on experiential ideas has recently been proposed by Kenton Anderson. Anderson argues that a multiplicity of sermon forms exists because human beings receive information in different ways. In this he is heavily influenced by the educational theories of David Kolb.[51] Kolb argues that there are two ways in which people receive information (either they are predominantly reflective receptors who observe or they are active and experiment) and two ways in which they input information (either they are abstract thinkers who need to conceptualize or they are concrete thinkers who need to experience). Elsewhere, Anderson has described the two axes as those of authority, which can be perceived objectively (by the reflective observer) or subjectively (by the active experimenter), and apprehension, which is achieved either cognitively (by the abstract thinkers) or intuitively (by the concrete thinkers).[52] This means, Anderson

---

48 *op. cit.*, vol. 1, p. 835.

49 *Design for Preaching*, p. vi.

50 M. Graves, *The Sermon as Symphony*, Valley Forge: Judson Press, 1997, p. 10.

51 *Choosing to Preach*, pp. 48f.

52 K. Anderson, *Preaching with Conviction: Connecting with Postmodern Listeners*, Grand Rapids: Kregel, 2001, p. 53.

(following Kolb) argues, that there are four sorts of learners, as each learner combines two elements, one from each axis (i.e., deductive/cognitive, inductive/cognitive, inductive/affective and deductive/affective).

If there are four different ways in which human beings learn about the world, then there are four ways in which human beings might be able to receive the message of the gospel. Different preachers have, therefore, spoken to some of their congregation more effectively than to others because of the various learning styles of the listeners. It is more than possible that among those who choose to worship in particular churches are those who do so because the style of preaching happens to be the one that feeds them (and this may certainly be the case for the North American Protestant Churches which Anderson has mainly in view), but it is also highly probable (especially in churches which are drawn together more by locality or denominational loyalty) that any given congregation on any Sunday will contain at least a few representatives of each learning style. More, it is possible that human beings are usually able to process information in one way but occasionally will find that another (less preferred) way is more effective. Studying contemporary preachers, Anderson concludes that the way in which they form their sermons has been to meet the listening needs of one of the four groups; for example, he argues that Eugene Lowry speaks more to those in the inductive/affective quadrant[53] and presumably (although Anderson does not make this point) least to those in the deductive/cognitive sector. Is it possible, Anderson therefore asks, to speak to all four quadrants at once? Certainly, a consistent preaching ministry could adopt forms that fit each of the four quadrants on successive Sundays, but Anderson wants to go further than that and proposes 'concurrent integration'.[54] A sermon can move systematically through the four quadrants of the Kolb/ Anderson grid. It would do this by successively 'telling the story' (which approximates to the inductive/affective quadrant), 'making a point' (deductive/affective), 'questioning the point' (deductive/

---

53 *Choosing to Preach*, p. 187.
54 *Choosing to Preach*, p. 253.

cognitive), and 'imagining the difference' (inductive/cognitive). However, working through a sermon, Anderson is careful to include within each section material which expresses ideas in deductive and inductive and affective and cognitive ways.

The Anderson grid works by moving around a central correlation between a biblical text and a contemporary image. An example of this is Anderson's sermon 'Unsolved Mysteries'.[55] The text is Colossians 1.24–29, and particularly some words from verse 27: 'this mystery, which is Christ in you'. He links this to modern mystery stories and to their conclusion; the central correlation is that Christ reveals the mystery of God as the author of detective fiction reveals the solution to the mystery in the final pages. Anderson's method is to work around this correlation, not revealing it until he is well into the second part of the sermon.

In the first quarter, Anderson tells the story, which is simply that 'life is full of mystery'. He engages the congregation with comments about the features of life that he finds mysterious (for example, modern technology) but moves to the bigger mysteries, the greatest of which is God, who he is and what he wants of us. There are two ways of dealing with mystery, Anderson avers: to solve it or to embrace it. In the second section, he makes his point – Jesus has solved the mystery. We live on the final page of the novel. The solution is that the fullness of God dwells in Christ (Col. 1.19) and Christ is in us. But (section three, questioning his point), part of him does not want to accept that. This is a particular concern of postmodernism, which argues that there are no ultimate answers but that we have to live with mystery. However, that means that life has no purpose. Secular postmodern philosophers accept that the only way out of this dilemma is to accept the existence of God, but some do not have the humility to do that. If one does (we move into section four, imagining the difference), we live with Christ and recognize that some mystery remains (most importantly, we can never understand why God

---

55 I am grateful to Dr Anderson for sending me an audio recording of this sermon. It is closely related to the material in *Preaching with Conviction*, pp. 123–41.

loves us), but we know all that we need to know, that God has revealed his love, hidden for ages, in Christ and therefore in us.

As Anderson consistently argues, in order to appeal to all four types of listener and to do justice to the text, there need to be four elements in the sermon; they need not always be presented in the same order, and in his most recent work Anderson has argued that as well as working logically through four quadrants, a preacher might move between the four elements throughout the sermon with a method that combines order and chaos ('chaordic').[56] This (which he also calls the 'concurrent integrative model') seems to be a work in progress and is not intended to be yet another form of sermon, but a suggestion to encourage practitioners to move freely between the four elements in their preaching.[57]

Anderson's concern is that preaching should speak to the postmodern listener and he engages with postmodern communication theory in order to achieve his goal. In this he is doing what Christian preachers in every age have done – finding ways to address their hearers in ways which they can receive. Whether or not the chaordic sermon is the next stage in that search remains to be seen; for now Anderson and those like him continue to preach and to think about the forms they use in preaching. In other words, the aim of twenty-first century preachers and homileticians remains to make the words acceptable.

---

56 *Choosing to Preach*, p. 255.

57 I am grateful to Dr Anderson for his clarification of this point in correspondence.

CONCLUSION

The world of the twenty-first-century preacher is a world far removed from that of John Chrysostom or the Venerable Bede. We might even argue that it is far removed from that of W. Edwin Sangster, who knew nothing of the internet or 24-hour television. It is not surprising that in such different ages the way in which sermons have been formed has differed. What is perhaps remarkable is how much the form of the sermon has remained recognizable. A preacher might as well simply comment verse by verse on a text and conclude with an exhortation to appropriate Christian action today as in the fourth century. This brief exploration of some of the forms that sermons have taken in history has shown that much of what seems at first sight to be confined to the past can be recovered and, with care, be used to present the message of the gospel in a way that has contemporary relevance. Preachers might be encouraged to consider working through a theme in the manner of the friars or approaching a sermon as if it were a letter, like John Henry Newman. If they were made available online, Charles Simeon's *Horae Homileticae* might even become an alternative to <www.desperatepreacher.com>.[1] It might be that a fuller study of historical forms of preaching would yield more possibilities that could be adapted for today, and there would be little surprising in that, because the goal of

---

1 A website that does exist.

the preacher has remained the same throughout the history of preaching. The Word made flesh is made words so that he might be received by his faithful people. Form still matters.

SELECT BIBLIOGRAPHY

Alan of Lille (tr. G. R. Evans), *The Art of Preaching* (Cistercian Studies 23), Kalamazoo: Cistercian Publications, 1981.

K. Anderson, *Preaching with Conviction: Connecting with Postmodern Listeners*, Grand Rapids: Kregel Publications, 2001.

—— *Preaching with Integrity*, Grand Rapids: Kregel Publications, 2003.

—— *Choosing to Preach*, Grand Rapids: Zondervan, 2006.

W. Boyd Carpenter, *Lectures on Preaching*, London & New York, 1895.

Bede (the Venerable) (tr. L. T. Martin and D. Hurst OSB), *Homilies on the Gospels*, 2 vols (Cistercian Studies 110 & 111), Kalamazoo: Cistercian Publications, 1991.

Tony Buzan with Barry Buzan, *The Mind Map Book*, rev. edn, London: BBC Publications, 2003.

Stephen Charnock, *A Discourse on the Pardon of Sin* published online: <http://www.puritansermons.com/charnock/charnoc6.htm>

John Chrysostom (tr. R. C. Hill), *Homilies on Genesis 1–17* (The Fathers of the Church, vol. 74), Washington DC: Catholic University of America Press.

—— *Homilies on Genesis 18–45* (The Fathers of the Church, vol. 82), Washington DC: Catholic University of America Press, 1990.

Fred Craddock, *Preaching*, Nashville: Abingdon, 1985.

—— *As One Without Authority*, rev. edn, St Louis: Chalice Press, 2001.

H. Grady Davis, *Design for Preaching*, Philadelphia: Fortress Press, 1958.

O. C. Edwards Jr, *A History of Preaching*, 2 vols, Nashville: Abingdon Press, 2004.

Mike Graves, *The Sermon as Symphony,* Valley Forge: Judson Press, 1997.

Richard Lischer (ed.), *The Company of Preachers: Wisdom on Preaching, Augustine to the Present*, Grand Rapids, Michigan and Cambridge, UK: Eerdmans, 2002.
E. L. Lowry, *The Homiletical Plot*, expanded edn, Louisville: Westminster, John Knox, 2001.

Wendy Mayer and Pauline Allen, *John Chrysostom*, London and New York: Routledge, 2000.

John Henry Newman, *Parochial and Plain Sermons*, 4th edn, 8 vols, London, 1844.
—— *The Idea of a University Defined and Illustrated*, London, 1907.
—— ed. I. Ker, *Apologia Pro Vita Sua*, London: Harmondsworth, 1990.
—— *Selected Sermons*, New York: Paulist Press, 1994.
—— ed. J. Tolhurst, *Sermon Notes of John Henry Cardinal Newman edited by the Fathers of the Birmingham Oratory*, Louisville: University of Notre Dame Press, 2000.

Hughes Oliphant Old, *The Reading and Preaching of the Scriptures in the Worship of the Christian Church*:
Vol. 1: The Biblical Period, Grand Rapids: Wm Eerdmans, 1998.
Vol. 2: The Patristic Age, Grand Rapids: Wm Eerdmans, 1998.
Vol. 3: The Medieval Church, Grand Rapids: Wm Eerdmans, 1999.
Vol. 4: The Age of the Reformation, Grand Rapids: Wm Eerdmans, 2002.
Vol. 5: Moderation, Pietism, and Awakening, Grand Rapids: Wm Eerdmans, 2004.

William Perkins (ed. S. B. Ferguson), *The Art of Prophesying with the Calling of the Ministry*, Edinburgh: Banner of Truth Trust, 1996, p. xii.

W. E. Sangster, *The Craft of Sermon Illustration*, London: Epworth Press, 1946.
—— *The Approach to Preaching*, London: Epworth Press, 1951.
—— *The Craft of Sermon Construction*, London: Epworth Press, 1954.

—— *Power in Preaching*, London: Epworth Press, 1958.

—— *Westminster Sermons*
   vol. 1: At Morning Worship, London: Epworth Press, 1960.
   vol. 2: At Fast and Festival, London: Epworth Press, 1961.

Charles Simeon, *Horae homileticae or, Discourses (principally in the form of skeletons) now first digested into one continued series and forming a commentary upon every book of the Old and New Testament to which is annexed, an improved edition of a translation of Claude's Essay on the composition of a sermon*, 21 volumes, London: Holdsworth and Ball, 1832–3.

C. M. Smith, *Weaving the Sermon: Preaching in a Feminist Perspective*, Louisville: Westminster John Knox, 1989.

Charles Smyth, *The Art of Preaching: A Practical Survey of Preaching in the Church of England 747–1939*, London, 1940.

Barbara Brown Taylor, *The Seeds of Heaven: Sermons on the Gospel of Matthew*, 2nd edn, Louisville: Westminster John Knox, 2004.

—— *When God is Silent*, Cambridge, Mass: Cowley Publications, 1997.

Simon Tugwell OP (ed.), *Early Dominicans: Selected Writings*, New York: Paulist Press, 1982.

John Wesley, *Works*, 3rd edn, London: Wesleyan Conference Office, 1872.

John Wilkins, *Ecclesiastes, or, A Discourse concerning the Gift of Preaching as it fals under the Rules of Art*, London, 1646.

John Wycliffe, *Sermones / now first edited from the manuscripts with critical and historical notes by Iohann Loserth (English side-notes by F. D. Matthew)*, London: Published for the Wyclif Society by Trübner, 1887–90.

INDEX